Penguin Education
Penguin English Project Stage One

Family and School
Edited by David Jackson

Chairman: Patrick Radley

Other Worlds
Edited by Donald Ball

Things Working
Edited by Penny Blackie

Family and School
Edited by David Jackson

Ventures
Edited by Elwyn Rowlands

I Took my Mind a Walk
Edited by George Sanders

Creatures Moving
Edited by Geoffrey Summerfield

Penguin English Project

Edited by David Jackson

Stage One **Family and School**

Penguin Books

For Dorothy

Penguin Books Ltd, Harmondsworth,
Middlesex, England
Penguin Books Australia Ltd, Ringwood,
Victoria, Australia

First published 1970
This selection copyright © David Jackson, 1970

Set in Monophoto Ehrhardt by
Oliver Burridge Filmsetting Ltd,
Crawley, England

Printed in Great Britain by
Fleming & Humphreys (Baylis) Ltd

Contents

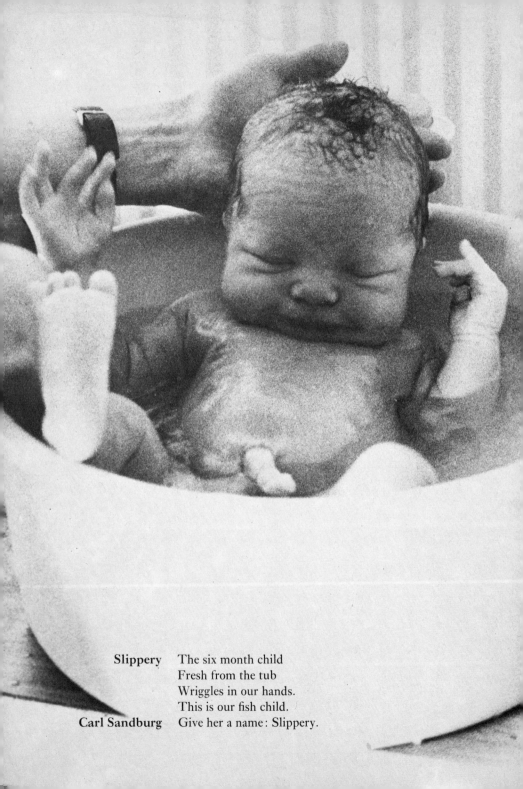

Slippery The six month child
Fresh from the tub
Wriggles in our hands.
This is our fish child.
Carl Sandburg Give her a name: Slippery.

Birth It was about five-thirty. Mrs Swann had left. The room looked squared up, Nan shut her eyes, so I went upstairs to where my two children were asleep. Marie stirred awake and spoke to me. She told me that she had dreamt of baby cries.

'Yes, you dreamt and you heard. Our baby has been born.'

'No? . . . honest, Dad? What is it?'

'A boy.'

'Larry, oh Larry!' she cried. 'Waken up! what do you think – baby has come! And it's a boy.'

'What's he like, Dad?'

'Well, he's not bad. Perhaps not so lovely as either of you . . . but I'm sure you'll like him. He's more beautiful than any baby except you two. He's big; Mrs Swann guessed he was more than nine pounds.'

I sat on Larry's bed. It was dark, but not black.

'Isn't it funny, Dad – he doesn't know what he's come to. He doesn't know I'm his brother, or that Marie's his sister.'

'I really wanted a girl, Dad; but now he's born I'm glad it's him, and that he's a boy.'

'I wonder what he'll think of us?'

'He'll like you – I'm sure he will.'

I gave a hand to each child.

'Now children, I must go to work this morning, and I want you to help while I'm away. I'll be back at dinner-time, it's Saturday. Your Mum must stay in bed; so what I want is for you to do some jobs – will you?'

'Yes, Dad.'

'Well, you Marie: I'd like you to make the tea for Mum if she wants it. Now you'll be sure to think of what you are doing. I mean, don't be talking or hurrying; but do it slowly and with thought. Then you're sure to do it right and you can't have an accident, and I won't be uneasy about you whilst at work. And I want you to do some shopping. I'll write it all down on a paper. If you're not sure, ask Mum; but don't ask her too many things. And I want both of you to watch for the coalman, and the milkman. Be ready at the door, so they don't rattle it. And keep the doors shut, or baby will catch a draught. I want you to wash yourselves well, and not forget your teeth . . .'

'But what about me, Dad? What jobs for me?'

'You, Larry, your job is to look after the fire. And to wash up. And if you remember, to peel potatoes for dinner. I want you to see there is quiet for Mum when she sleeps. But one thing you must promise me: not to stay in the house all morning. You must go out.'

'Yes, Dad.'

'And now, you two sausages – listen: oatmeal is in the small blue pan, it will be cooked, and only needs warming for breakfast. And there'll be fat for fried bread in the frying pan. Heat it like I showed you, use a fork, don't dip the bread till it's hot. Kiss now, God bless. Go to sleep my loves and I'll wake you as I'm leaving for work.'

'I'll remember, Dad.'

'Me, too, Dad. I'll look after the fire.'

'Stay a bit longer, Dad . . . talk to us.'

A Roof over Your Head
Bill Naughton
'Well, not just now. I must go to baby and Mum. Good night, Marie. Good night, Larry.'

Riddle *What goes into the water yellow and comes out of it white?*

Seeing a Parent Cry for the First Time
I was only eight at the time and that morning my mother seemed quite happy and cheerful. I was all ready for school when my Dad came rushing in; he seemed in a terrible flap.

I said, 'Good-bye Mum.'

There was no answer, only a lot of muffled talk.

I said again, 'Good-bye Dad.'

There was still no answer so I walked out to catch the bus.

It was a long day and the classroom was stuffy. I couldn't work in the heat and I was glad when it was time to go home. When the bus got home, I went in and Mum and Dad weren't in. I got changed and went to sit in the garden. It was too hot to play football with the lads and too hot to sit and play with dolls or go roller-skating with the girls, so I walked about.

When I got back home my Mum was sitting in the kitchen. She was looking miserable and very tired. I asked her what was wrong.

'Oh nothing. Your tea's on the table.'

'I know. I thought . . .'

'Well you know what thought did.'

'Oh well if you're in that sort of mood.'

I went to the table and started my tea. As I had just finished Dad walked in the door. He was pale and looked very ill.

'What's the matter Dad?' I said.

He walked straight past me as if he hadn't seen me.

I finished my tea and went out. I thought that was the best way.

After about half an hour I decided that I wanted to watch T.V. so I walked home. As I walked through the door my Dad was standing with his face to the wall, and Mum was sitting there crying her eyes out. It was the first time I had ever seen her cry, and I immediately stopped thinking of her as a great lady that no one or nothing could hurt.

As I went over to her I looked at her and talked to her in a voice that she always talked to me in when I was hurt. She managed a little smile but then broke down and cried again. She took hold of me and said, 'I'll never let it happen to you.'

I was puzzled but I didn't say anything for I knew questions would hurt her all the more.

When Dad turned round he looked ill and old. All my dreams of him being my hero in shining armour dropped as well. I never knew what had happened but it hurt me too, because now I knew I couldn't depend on them as much as I could before, when I knew they could be hurt too.

Age 13
Carole Carr

Five Green Bottles An ordinary household. The play is set in the kitchen which is roomy, and leads into the hall and living-room. The time of the play is that time of rush between 8 o'clock and 8.45 a.m. on any weekday.

> *[Gramp is reading the paper. Kevin is eating his toast. The radio is blaring cheery music. Mother is in the hall – calling upstairs]*

MOTHER David! It's eight o'clock. Are you coming down or aren't you! David!

DAVID *[Upstairs]* All right!

MOTHER No 'all right' about it! Do you hear me!

DAVID *[Low]* Keep your hair on.

MOTHER *[Going up a couple of steps]* What did you say?

DAVID I'm combing me hair down.

MOTHER We'll have less of your lip, my lad. And I'm not calling you again. You'll be late. And tell that Maureen as well. *[Coming down the steps]* Talk about a house of the dead.

DAVID *[Hammering on a door]* Maureen!

MOTHER *[Shouting]* There's no need to shout!

DAVID *[Singing]* Maureen-O!

MOTHER Maureen, you'll be late! *[Pause]*

DAVID She's died in her sleep.

MOTHER I give up.

> *[She comes back into the kitchen]*

Nobody can get up in this house – you must get it from your father. If I slept half as much as you lot do there'd be nothing done –

KEVIN The world'd fall to bits –

MOTHER Kevin – get that telescope off the table –

KEVIN I'm looking at tomato cells.

GRAMP This paper's all creased!

MOTHER Don't moan, Dad!

GRAMP It's like trying to read an elephant's knee-cap!

MOTHER Why've you left that piece of bacon?

KEVIN It's all fat.

MOTHER You don't know what's good for you – it keeps out the cold –

KEVIN Why don't they make coats out of it then?

MOTHER That's enough. And turn that music down for heaven's sake – you can't even hear yourself think in a din like that.

KEVIN It's supposed to make you feel bright and breezy.

MOTHER You must be joking. Turn it off.

[The radio is switched off]

Oh! A bit of peace at last!

GRAMP Never had bacon when I went to school, never had bacon and . . . and . . . and what're the other things?

KEVIN Eggs.

MOTHER Now don't go on about it, Dad.

GRAMP Aye, eggs. Never. Just bread and jam and a four-mile walk.

KEVIN Aren't you glad you came to live with us then?

MOTHER Kevin, that's enough of that! There's a lot you youngsters today have to be thankful for and a full stomach's one of them.

GRAMP Just bread and jam and a five-mile walk.

KEVIN Four you said.

GRAMP It might've been six if you count the hills.

MOTHER There's many a starving Chinese who'd be only too glad to finish what you leave.

KEVIN Show me one.

MOTHER Kevin, how many more times!

GRAMP Where're my glasses? I can't read without my glasses.

KEVIN The cat's wearing them.

MOTHER Kevin!

GRAMP It's a plot!

MOTHER Oh I don't know. If it's not one it's the other. What've I done wrong O Lord!

GRAMP The words go up and down without them.

MOTHER *[Patiently]* Where did you have them last, Dad?

GRAMP I had them just now.

MOTHER Are you sitting on them?

GRAMP Don't be daft – why should I sit on them?

MOTHER Stranger things have happened. Get up. Come on. Get up.

[Gramp gets up. He's been sitting on them]

There you are. What did I say?

GRAMP Who put them there, that's what I'd like to know!

KEVIN *[Low]* The cat.

MOTHER Do you want any more tea?

KEVIN No, thanks.

GRAMP Look, they're all twisted. You've got to have a head like a corkscrew to get them on now!

MOTHER *[Calling]* David! Maureen! I won't tell you again! It's ten past eight already!

GRAMP *[Reading out the headlines]* 'BERLIN TABLE TALKS'. *[He giggles]* Do you get it, young Kevin?

KEVIN Loud and clear.

GRAMP Berlin table – talks!

KEVIN *[Low]* Very funny!

GRAMP What d'you say?

KEVIN *[Loud]* Very funny.

GRAMP Aye. *[Mournfully]* Nobody laughs nowadays. That's the trouble with the world.

MOTHER What were you and David quarrelling about last night?

KEVIN Nothing.

MOTHER Nobody makes noise like that about nothing. Your dad's only got one ear and he heard it too. What was it?

KEVIN Nothing. *[He gets up]*

MOTHER Where're you going?

KEVIN Get my books.

MOTHER You still haven't answered my question, young man!

KEVIN It was nothing – honest.

MOTHER Talk about blood from a stone. And take this telescope – I've only got one pair of hands.
[Letters come in through the front door]
There's the post.
[A door slams upstairs]

DAVID I'll get them.

MOTHER No, let David do it – it'll be one way of getting him

KEVIN I'll get them.

MOTHER No, let David do it – it'll be one way of getting him downstairs.
[David is rushing downstairs]

KEVIN It's always him.
[The living-room door slams]

MOTHER *[Concerned]* I hope it's about our Maureen's job. If it's not, she'll be so cut up.

GRAMP 'RENEWED FIGHTING IN SOUTH EAST ASIA'. It never stops.

MOTHER I don't think it ever will.

GRAMP What's that?

MOTHER War.

GRAMP You and the boys are always fighting—

MOTHER That's different.

GRAMP Same drink, bigger bottle.
[David comes slowly from the hall]

DAVID One for Dad . . . one for Gramp. And the pools thing.
[Pause]

MOTHER Nothing for our Maureen?

DAVID No, I looked.

[Pause]

MOTHER Well, let's keep our fingers crossed and hope something comes in the second post.

DAVID Here you are, Gramp.

GRAMP For me? [Afraid] Who's writing to me! I bet it's money they're after –

MOTHER Well, open it up and see.

GRAMP I'm a pensioner, not the Bank of England.

MOTHER You've got enough to sink a battleship.

GRAMP A punt, maybe, but not a battleship.

[A door slams upstairs]

MOTHER Oh, those doors!

MAUREEN Is that the post?

MOTHER Yes.

MAUREEN My letter there?

MOTHER No, love. Nothing.

[Pause]

MAUREEN Oh.

[Pause]

Too bad.

MOTHER It might come with the second post, love.

MAUREEN Pigs might fly an' all.

MOTHER Now there's no call to think like that. I don't want you to give up.

MAUREEN Oh, I'll be all right.

[A door slams upstairs]

MOTHER Those doors ! ! ! [Calling] And hurry up.

MAUREEN I am!

MOTHER Poor girl. She'd set her heart on that job.

DAVID What job?

MOTHER If you'd pay attention to your sister for once in a while you'd know what job.

DAVID She don't think of us!

MOTHER Do you want an egg?

DAVID How can you go to work on an egg – it'd crack.

MOTHER I asked you a simple, straightforward question.

DAVID No thanks, just cereal.

MOTHER At last!

[Cereal is shaken into a bowl]

and help yourself to milk.

[Kevin enters]

KEVIN Where've you put my books!

DAVID [Mouth full] Nowhere.

KEVIN Come on—

DAVID Leave go! I haven't touched them!

KEVIN That's just the sort of dirty—

DAVID Watch it—

KEVIN Where did you put my books!

MOTHER Will you two stop it!

KEVIN He's been and—

MOTHER I mean it!

> [Silence]
>
> Now let's get this straight once and for all. If you two can't get up in the morning without tearing each other's hair out – then at least have some consideration for other people.

GRAMP Like hiding their glasses.

MOTHER I'm doing the talking, dad. There're others in this house besides you. And I mean it. Now, both of you, hurry up and get out of my sight before I do something I'll be sorry for.

> [She breaks an egg into a frying pan. It misses]
>
> Oh no! Quick, Kevin, a rag!
>
> [Kevin's chair scrapes]

KEVIN Use this!

MOTHER [Upset] Oh, look at it! All over the side! That's what comes of listening to you two.

KEVIN Sorry, mum.

MOTHER It's all spoilt.

> [Pause]

DAVID I didn't want an egg.

MOTHER It wasn't for you – it was for that Maureen.

KEVIN Do you know where my books are, Mum?

MOTHER Mum, Mum, Mum – am I supposed to know everything?

KEVIN No, but—

MOTHER [Forced calm] If they're with the pinkish one with not many pages then they're on the television.

DAVID You put them there before 'Z-Cars'.

KEVIN Why don't you drop dead.

DAVID Dad can't afford the coffin.

KEVIN Pity.

MOTHER On your way – and call that Maureen – she'll be late sure as eggs.

KEVIN Joke.

MOTHER What does that mean?

KEVIN Eggs – sure as eggs.

MOTHER *[Dawning]* Oh, very funny – get a move on!

[Kevin goes into the hall]

KEVIN Hey – longlegs!

MAUREEN *[Upstairs]* What?

KEVIN It's twenty-to. If you hurry up, you'll just be half-hour late.

MAUREEN I *am* hurrying.

KEVIN Mum's gone.

MAUREEN Where?

KEVIN Rest home. Two little blokes in white coats're dragging her screaming out the back into an ambulance.

MAUREEN Very clever.

KEVIN It's a quarter-to.

MAUREEN It's not half-past!

[Kevin comes into the kitchen]

KEVIN She's alive.

MOTHER Here's your tea.

KEVIN Ta.

MOTHER Thank you, not ta.

KEVIN *[Overdoing it]* From the heart of my bottom – I thank you dear mother.

MOTHER Oh, what's the use?

GRAMP *[Shouting with wonder and excitement]* They want me to play!

KEVIN Who – England?

MOTHER Kevin!

GRAMP Bowls!

KEVIN Never heard of 'em.

GRAMP Kathy – they want me to bowl. Me!

MOTHER When?

GRAMP *[Awe-struck]* Tomorrow.

MOTHER That's very nice. I'm glad. It'll mean a nice break for you, a change from just sitting around here.

GRAMP It's an . . . honour.

MOTHER Of course it is.

GRAMP After all . . . I'm new to the game.

MOTHER Dan says you're very good.

GRAMP You know, I never thought I'd do it!

MOTHER If you don't stop jigging up and down you won't be able to – what're you sniggering at!

KEVIN Nothing.

GRAMP I'll have to get ready.

MOTHER But it's not till tomorrow!

GRAMP *[Excited]* What about my whites?

MOTHER They're clean.

GRAMP And pressed?

MOTHER And pressed.

GRAMP They must be . . . knife edge. And my blazer? And my cravat? And my white pullover? And my handkerchief with the works crest on?

MOTHER They're all ready, love.

GRAMP And my hockey cap.

MOTHER You can't wear that! *[Pause]*

GRAMP Right, I think I'll go and clean my shoes—

MOTHER Dad, they're like mirrors already.

GRAMP I must be ready. And I'll have an early night to be on the safe side.

MOTHER *[laughing]* But it's still early morning.

GRAMP I'm very . . . happy, my dear.

[He goes out]

DAVID *[Whispering]* He's crying!

MOTHER *[Quietly]* It means a lot to him.

KEVIN Why?

MOTHER Just . . . because he's an old man.

[Pause]

[Calling] And give that Maureen a shake, Dad.

[But the old man is singing 'Underneath the Lamplight' and doesn't hear her]

What're you so quiet about?

DAVID Can I have a black shirt, Mum?

KEVIN Here we go.

DAVID Shut up, you!

KEVIN Watch it!

DAVID Watch it yourself!

MOTHER You two!

[Silence]

Why? Why do you want a black shirt?

DAVID *[Low]* 'Cos . . . I want one.

MOTHER And you always get what you want.

DAVID No.

DAVID Why then?

KEVIN 'Cos everybody else's got one!

MOTHER I didn't ask you.

DAVID *[Helplessly]* 'Cos I . . . just want one.

MOTHER And you've got to be like everybody else, I suppose.

DAVID No.

KEVIN Yes.

DAVID No.

MOTHER Oh, stop it, both of you. I can't be bothered with that now. Off to school, you'll be late.

[Pause]

DAVID *[Persistent]* Can I have one?

MOTHER No.

DAVID Why not?

MOTHER It all costs money, that's why not. When I cough, three-penny bits don't drop out, you know.

DAVID All our lot in the form've got them.

[Kevin baas like a sheep]

MOTHER I bought you a new white one only the other week. I'm not made of money. School rules say white shirts not black.

DAVID It's not for school!

MOTHER No need to raise your voices. Besides, you've got other shirts for best and for knocking around—

DAVID It's not for knocking around in.

MOTHER Then what's it for?

[Gramp is now singing 'Marching through Georgia' tunelessly]

Come on, tell me.

DAVID I just *want* one.

KEVIN To wear to Gerry's.

MOTHER Gerry's what?

KEVIN Party, Friday.

MOTHER And all the others'll have them as well I suppose – you'll only want Mussolini there and you can start the Third World War.

DAVID I don't know what you're on about.

MOTHER *[Softly]* No – I don't suppose you do.

DAVID Then can I have one?

MOTHER No. And that's final.

[Pause]

You'll have to see your father.

[David bangs his teacup down]

DAVID It's always the same!

[Enter Maureen in a hurry, in high heels]

MAUREEN What is?

DAVID Nothing.

MAUREEN Do you know Gramp's cleaning his shoes on the landing? There's bits of black all over the wall.

MOTHER Anything can happen this morning.

MAUREEN Is that the time?

MOTHER No, it's midnight. I've made you an egg—

MAUREEN No, only tea.

MOTHER Maureen!

MAUREEN I'm sorry, I haven't got time.

MOTHER And who's fault's that – you never eat.

MAUREEN I'm all right.

[*A cup is passed*]

That way I won't get fat. Ta.

DAVID Don't say ta, say thank you.

MAUREEN What's up with you all of a sudden?

DAVID Nothing.

MAUREEN More milk, Mum, please, it's too hot.

MOTHER David wants a black shirt. I can't afford it, neither can
your father. He works hard enough as it is – he's got a
family and a father to keep and that's strain enough on what
he earns.

MAUREEN [*Sipping*] Oh, that's better. Oh, buy him one – or
it'll be a guitar and bongo-drums next time.

MOTHER I've told you, I'm not made of—

DAVID [*Upset*] All right!

MAUREEN He never asks for anything, Mum, so this must be
important if he asks for it.

MOTHER I don't like disappointing anybody—

DAVID All right!

MOTHER But as it is I can't afford it!

MAUREEN Skip it.

MOTHER If it's that important, why don't you buy it?

MAUREEN [*Half angry*] If I'd got that job I could afford it and
I would.

DAVID I DON'T WANT IT NOW!

[*Silence*]

MAUREEN [*Softly*] How much are they?

DAVID I don't want it.

MAUREEN Forty bob?

[*Silence*]

Come on silly.

DAVID I don't *want* it.

[*Pause*]

KEVIN [*Low*] Twenty-five.

MAUREEN All right then.

[*Pause*]

DAVID You will?

MAUREEN Why not? Money comes, money goes. At least it'll
make one person happy.

DAVID I'll pay you back half-a-crown a week.

MAUREEN Don't make promises.

DAVID I will.

MAUREEN Then we'll get it tonight.

MOTHER You don't have to give in to him, you know.

MAUREEN Perhaps I want to.

MOTHER It's your money.

MAUREEN What about you, Kev? Do you want one as well?

DAVID *[Going into the hall]* He won't, he said they're mad.

KEVIN *[Surly]* I didn't.

DAVID You did last night!

KEVIN That was different!

MOTHER So that's what all the noise was about.
> *[Pause]*

MAUREEN Well, Kev? I haven't got all day.

KEVIN Can I have one too, please?
> *[David baas like a sheep in the hall]*
> I'll thump you.

DAVID You're not big enough, ugly enough or old enough.

KEVIN Wanna try?

MOTHER You two – out!
> *[They are both in the hall]*

KEVIN Thanks, Maur.

MAUREEN Pleasure.

MOTHER And don't forget your caps – you know what happened last time.

DAVID Thanks, Maur. Cheerio, Mum. Cheerio, Gramp!

MOTHER Mind that door!
> *[It slams]*
> Talk to the wall.
> *[Gramp starts singing 'Ten Green Bottles' on the stairs]*
> It only needs Dad to start!

MAUREEN Change from his moaning. What's he so happy about?

MOTHER He's in the bowling team tomorrow. Have you got time for another cup?

MAUREEN I wonder who got that job.

MOTHER Stop fretting.

MAUREEN Who's fretting? I just feel I'm doing nothing where I am, that's all. I'm useless. Don't know why they keep me. They must like my legs.

MOTHER Maureen!

MAUREEN I'll just have to get married. And have quads. Four lots.

MOTHER I wish you'd eat something.

MAUREEN I'll have a doughnut come eleven.

MOTHER [*Fondly*] One minute she's talking of slimming, the next she's eating doughnuts . . .

MAUREEN [*In the clouds*] I shall die . . . in my bed . . . surrounded by half-nibbled doughnuts. . . .

MOTHER I don't want to rush you, but it's gone twenty-to.

MAUREEN Oh, let them wait. I'm fed up.

MOTHER Maureen!

MAUREEN Come on, put your feet up, I only sit around till ten anyway.

[*Chairs scrape*]

MOTHER Oh, what it is to get your feet up!

MAUREEN I never do anything else.

MOTHER It was nice of you – about those shirts.

MAUREEN Why?

MOTHER Well, it obviously meant a lot to our David.

MAUREEN I know.

MOTHER Those two baffle me sometimes. You all do, come to that. Kids. You have them, you raise them and then, one day, before you can turn round, you don't know them. They might as well be Zulus.

MAUREEN 'The trouble with parents is they don't listen to what their children say.'

MOTHER Very clever.

MAUREEN Some things're . . . important.

MOTHER Like black shirts?

MAUREEN Might be.

MOTHER Then God help the world.

MAUREEN Our David's just twelve. He's changing . . . that's why he's always doing his hair, why they fight, why they hate caps . . . why they want tapered trousers – why they collect records. It's all necessary. If they were Zulus – they'd . . . I don't know – they'd be out killing a buffalo. To prove themselves. It's bound to happen.

MOTHER Quite a philosopher!

MAUREEN [*Softly*] I'd give them anything . . . anything as long as they don't end up . . . just filling in petrol checks. Like me.

[*Pause. She gets up*]

I'm off. It's going to rain.

MOTHER It had to happen. I only cleaned the windows yesterday.

[*Gramp enters*]

GRAMP Here. Found this by the front door. It's for you, Maureen.

MOTHER Letter!

MAUREEN It might be—

  [Letter is torn open. Pause]

  I've got it! I've got the job!

MOTHER Well, don't strangle me.

GRAMP Thought it might have been important.

MAUREEN All the world's pink! Start next Tuesday.

MOTHER There, what did I say!

GRAMP You playing bowls too then?

MAUREEN Do you want a black shirt as well, Gramp, while I'm at it?

GRAMP You must be mad.

MAUREEN I am.

GRAMP I always knew there was something about this house.

MOTHER *[Pleased]* Come on - hurry up, you've still got this job to finish.

MAUREEN See you then!

MOTHER Out!

MAUREEN You smell of fried bread!

MOTHER Out! And mind that door!

MAUREEN 'Bye, Gramp.

  [The door slams. Pause]

GRAMP She didn't hear you.

MOTHER Peace at last. It's like the Armistice when they've gone.

GRAMP And then there was one.

MOTHER One what?

GRAMP Green bottle.

MOTHER You're as mad as the rest of them. One day, they'll all come down those stairs on time, they'll all eat together and quietly and they'll all leave . . . *closing* the door behind them. Early.

GRAMP If they did you wouldn't know what to do with yourself.

MOTHER I'd die of shock, Dad, I know that for a fact. Stark staring shock.

  [Gramp begins to sing 'Ten Green Bottles']

  Come on, out from under my feet. I've got this place to clean for when the hordes return –

GRAMP I hope it doesn't rain . . .

MOTHER It will.

GRAMP I can't bowl when the green's wet. Blast!

MOTHER Now what's up?

Ray Jenkins GRAMP *[Like a child]* I can't find my glasses.

**If a man
who turnips cries**

Anonymous

If a man who turnips cries,
Cry not when his father dies
It is a proof that he would rather
Have a turnip than his father.

Spilling Soup

*[Albert Schearl has brought Luter, a friend from work, back to
have some tea but Albert's son, David, is very shy.]*

'What's the matter with him?' asked his father sharply.

'I don't quite know. Perhaps his stomach. He has eaten very
little today.'

'Well, he'll eat now,' said his father warningly. 'You feed him
too many trifles.'

'A doubtful stomach is a sad thing,' said Luter condoningly, and David hated him for his sympathy.

'Ach,' exclaimed his father, 'it isn't his stomach, Joe, it's his palate – jaded with delicacies.'

His mother set the soup before him. 'This will taste good,' she coaxed.

He dared not refuse, though the very thought of eating sickened him. Steeling himself against the first mouthful, he dipped the spoon into the shimmering red liquid, lifted it to his lips. Instead of reaching his mouth, the spoon reached only his chin, struck against the hollow under his lower lip, scalded it, fell from his nerveless fingers into the plate. A red fountain splashed out in all directions, staining his blouse, staining the white tablecloth. With a feeling of terror David watched the crimson splotches on the cloth widen until they met each other.

His father lowered his spoon angrily into his plate.

'Lame as a Turk!' he snapped, rapping the table with his knuckles. 'Will you lift your head, or do you want that in the plate too?'

He raised frightened eyes. Luter glanced at him sideways, sucking his teeth in wary disapproval.

'It's nothing!' exclaimed his mother comfortingly. 'That's what tablecloths were made for.'

'To splash soup on, eh?' retorted her husband sarcastically. 'And that's what shirts were made for too! Very fine. Why not the whole plate while he's at it?'

Luter chuckled.

Without answering, his mother reached over and stroked his brow with her palm. 'Go on and eat, child.'

'What are you doing now,' demanded his father, 'sounding his brow for fever? Child! There's absolutely nothing wrong with the brat, except your pampering him!' He shook his finger at David ominously. 'Now you swill your soup like a man, or I'll ladle you out something else instead.'

Henry Roth

Proverb *One father is worth more than a hundred Schoolmasters.*

The Cruel Mother

There was a lady lived in York,
    All alone and a loney,
A farmer's son he courted her,
    All down by the greenwood sidey.

He courted her for seven long years.
At last she proved in child by him.

She pitched her knee against a tree,
And there she found great misery.

She pitched her back against a thorn,
And there she had her baby born.

She drew the fillet off her head,
She bound the baby's hands and legs.

She drew a knife both long and sharp
She pierced the baby's innocent heart.

She wiped the knife upon the grass,
The more she wiped, the blood run fast.

She washed her hands all in the spring,
Thinking to turn a maid again.

As she was going to her father's hall,
She saw three babes a playing at ball.

One dressed in silk, the other in satin,
The other star-naked as ever was born.

O, dear baby, if you was mine,
I'd dress you in silk and satin so fine.

O, dear mother, I once was thine
You never would dress me coarse or fine.

The coldest earth it was my bed
The green grass was my coverlet.

O, mother, mother, for your sin,
Heaven gate you shall not enter in.

There is a fire beyond hell's gate,
Traditional English And there you'll burn both early and late.

32

The Best Room

The best room smelt of moth balls and fur and damp and dead plants and stale, sour air. Two glass cases on wooden coffin-boxes lined the window wall. You looked at the weed-grown vegetable garden through a stuffed fox's legs, over a partridge's head, along the red-paint-stained breast of a stiff wild duck. A case of china and pewter, trinkets, teeth, family brooches,

Dylan Thomas

stood beyond the bandy table.

Riddle

Why did the coal scuttle?

The Cupboard under the Stairs

There was another good hide-out in our house – the cupboard under the front stairs. It was full of old clothes and baskets of rags, shoe-boxes full of papers and broken toys. When the door was shut, I found myself in total darkness, enjoying my utter privacy and the intimate human smell of old hats and clothes. I would sit in the blackness on the old creaky washing basket and press my fingers hard upon my eyeballs to produce swirling patterns of stars, suns, blazing moons and comets, brilliant dots and dashes of purple and red that switched suddenly to yellow and lurid green. In the singing silence of these self-induced visions I would be startled to hear distant voices and very high music. Sometimes I heard animals growling and grunting and barking, and birds bellowing out of trees full of roaring wind. As the shapes and colours in my tight pressed eyes began to explode more and more violently into riots of fireworks the voices would begin to detonate like huge, banging bells or waves thumping the hard-packed

Sorrows, Passions and Alarms
James Kirkup

beaches of a stormy sea. I got a bit frightened then, and quietly uttering my favourite exclamation, 'Mlaa!' I would rush out of the cupboard into the real sun of the front door.

Proverb

Better a snotty child, than his nose wiped off.

The Vacuum

The house is so quiet now
The vacuum cleaner sulks in the corner closet,
Its bag limp as a stopped lung, its mouth
Grinning into the floor, maybe at my
slovenly life, my dog-dead youth.

I've lived this way long enough,
But when my old woman died her soul
Went into that vacuum cleaner, and I can't bear
To see the bag swell like a belly, eating the dust
And the woollen mice, and begin to howl.

Because there is old filth everywhere
She used to crawl, in the corner and under the stair.
I know now how life is cheap as dirt,
And still the hungry, angry heart
Hangs on and howls, biting at air.

Howard Nemerov

Riddle

What did the big tap say to the little tap?

**What a Blessing
Younger Brothers Are**

When my sister says to me,
'Go and put the kettle on,'
I say to my younger brother,
'Go and put the kettle on,'
So my brother goes and puts the kettle on.

When my younger brother says to me,
'Bring a tin of fruit up,'
I say to my elder sister,
'Bring a tin of fruit up,'
But she says,
'Go yourself you lazy thing,'
So I say to my younger brother,
'Go yourself you lazy thing!'
So he goes and brings the tin of fruit up.

Age 13
Catherine Frankland

Haiku
*Translated from the
Japanese by
Geoffrey Bownas and
Anthony Thwaite*
Anonymous

Making her doll
Play younger sister –
The only child.

Dressing Up   Kathleen and I were playing dressing up. Kathleen's brother,
Ian, and my brother, Bernard, were playing somewhere down
at Gran's. We were glad, as we didn't want them fussing
around us. We went nearly to Kathleen's house, but still on
Grandad's land. As we walked along the corner of the field we
kept down in case the lads saw us, because they said we were
stupid and cissies. But we enjoyed ourselves though, daubing
ourselves with make-up, and wearing dresses much too long
for us. It was an afternoon with sun beaming and bouncing off
our already sunburnt faces. Kathleen's freckles were hardly
noticeable.

We dawdled, putting on our make-up, dresses and shoes as the
sun was rather hot. We decided to have our work, 'the office'
as it always was, down the field a bit where, at the side of the
field was the fence with a thorn tree in front with a branch to
sit on. But as we began to walk to work leaving a bag with
two coats and dresses in behind, a refreshing wind began to

blow coolly on our hot brown faces, and in a posh voice Kathleen began saying, 'It's rather a cool breeze blowing, isn't it, this morning?' My reply was, 'Yes come on,' getting less posh 'Let's run.'

We did and found it clumsy running with handbags, so we threw them up in the air and they fell on the ground with a bang. It was difficult trying to run with the shoes too. I first kicked one leg in the air, and the shoe came off, then the other. Kathleen decided to do the same.

We tripped over our dresses but we didn't care and we ran to the bottom of the field in our stocking feet. We were enjoying ourselves, laughing and breathless.

As we walked up the field we picked up our shoes and handbags. Laughing and breathing hard, we slumped down on the grass next to the bag with the dresses in.

'Wonder where the lads are?' said Kathleen when we had regained our senses.

'Wouldn't have the faintest,' I replied dreamily.

'Ha, ha!' – the lads. Kathleen and I screamed. They were armed with sticks and soil bombs – little mudballs which contained a small stone.

'Look, leave us alone, we haven't got any ammunition,' I flared.

We glanced round for any object we could find. They threw soil bombs and hit us with their sticks. I threw a stick and it hit Ian and made him cry. I wished I hadn't thrown it.

'I never hurt you,' I said, wishing I hadn't said it.

'You have, he's crying,' said Bernard.

At which he hit me so hard with sticks I really did cry. Then as Kathleen was telling the lads off, I heard Kathleen scream, and looked round to see if they had hit her, but no, then a tap on my finger and a graze down my shin. It was a fairly big piece of rotten wood. I pretended to cry, and the lads went. Kathleen thought I really was crying. They went but kept muttering, 'You're soft.'

When they had gone, Kathleen said, 'Are you all right?' She discovered I was, and started laughing, so did I. We buried our faces in the grass, and exhausted ourselves with all the laughing.

Age 12
Helen Wills

Many, many hours of my childhood were spent in learning how to whistle. In learning how to snap my fingers. In hanging from the branch of a tree. In looking at an ants' nest. In digging holes. Making piles. Tearing things down. Throwing rocks at things.

Spitting. Breaking sticks in half. . . . And we made slides on the sidewalk and damn near broke our necks, and then some grown-ups came out and spread ashes on it, and we grumbled.

Robert Paul Smith

At a sweetshop and stationers someone started a craze for buying flat boxes of six (was it?) Anadin tablets, dissolving them in water in a small bottle of aspirin size, and drinking the pink liquid as though it were lemonade or some other children's beverage.

B. S. Johnson

Later, when scooters got too babyish and a soap-box trolley was the rage I nagged at somebody to make me one. Then it was a matter of finding the right spot, a quiet hill, a strip of deserted pavement and some means of slowing down at the bottom. This was the car world now, it was a car town where even the workers have cars of their own, so naturally we needed soap-box cars for playing in. You sat there in state on the plank and pram wheels, the axle swivelled under the feet by tow cords which you held in your hands and tugged as if you held horse reins. On waste ground where the grass had been worn off it was a free, hectic, bumping ride, and on a gentle slope of pavement it was slow and oiled, majestic. Certain streets had special atmospheres. Hampton Street for instance – long, quiet and gradual, ideal for a trolley, right near home, so you could nip out before tea was ready, straight after school, gliding down slowly, gathering speed, hearing the regular bump-bump as the cast iron covers of the pavement gutters ran under the wheels – at the bottom grabbing the reins and

Philip Callow   charging up again to the top for just one more ride.

One of the most exciting things you could spend a penny on was a box of caps, either singles – confetti with blobs of bang in the middle – or rolls, for Buffalo Bill six-shooters. We used the singles also in a rather frightening weapon called a bomb – a miniature hand grenade consisting of two portions of grooved metal held together by a length of twine: you put a cap between the portions, tightened the twine, threw the bomb into the air, and it came down on the pavement with a cracking explosion.

Clifford Dyment

Another enthusiasm at the same time was a secret society I formed with Batesy. It had its headquarters in a certain tree, difficult to climb, but low, hawthorn I think it must have been, where we hid all kinds of formulae, little bottles of pink Anadin mixture, matches and other valuables. Two other kids we allowed to belong to this society, who were not very enthusiastic, who did not turn up to meetings very often: when Batesy and I saw them once some weeks later they did not even seem to remember belonging. But someone found all the things in H.Q., robbed us, and we found these two and accused them: they denied betraying the society, but we thumped them, just in case.

B. S. Johnson

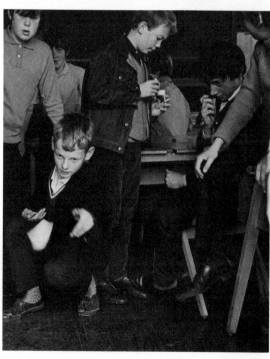

Door-Knocking   We started to play a new sort of knock down ginger.

We no longer just knocked at doors and ran. Instead we tied
the hanging doorknockers of houses together with wireless wire
which is so thin it can't be noticed unless it flashes in the sun;
to and fro we tied it, across and across, up and down the
street. Then we sat in the alley and waited.

Mrs Murdoe would open her door for the morning milk. This
would cause Mrs Grindle's knocker to rattle. Out would come
Mrs Grindle with her Pleased-to-welcome-all-commercial-
travellers look all over her toothy yellow face; only she would
find no one there. Back out again would come Mrs Murdoe,
annoyed at hearing the knocker go as soon as she left the front
door and wearing a horrid look so the man would know she did
not want any boot brushes. She would fling the door open with
a crash and glare round; then she would go back in with
another crash, disappointed at not being able to have a
slanging match. This would start several doors going.

Out would come Mrs Plumber, quick for a chat, only no one to
chat with; Mrs Harty, tucking herself into her dress and
shaking all over; Mrs Rate, kicking the cat; Mrs Holland
moaning all the way along the hall, 'Oh, dear me, oh dear me,
dear, dear', to stand and pant and then sneeze at the front door.

That was only the start, because by now all the doors would be
banging and knocking, banging and knocking, opening and
closing. Dragon knockers, gnome knockers, plain knockers,
wooden knockers, Mrs Murdoe's knocker which knocked with a
brass mermaid's bottom, Mrs Swan's knocker which knocked
a hole in a rotten door.

Out they would come, muttering and coughing, swearing,
scolding, angry, perplexed, dressed and undressed; then the fun
would start.

'It's them kids; it's them blasted kids!'

'Why don't you keep yourn in, Mrs Murdoe?'

'Mine are in, Dot.'

'Os's that, then – laughin' under the 'edge?'

Then up would come the window of the local scold: 'Why
don't yer stop yer bleedin' row?'

'Ree-lee!'

'Dear me!'

'That woman!'

Deaf Mrs Murphy down the street, 'What does she say?'

'She says . . .'

'I bleedin' well said why don't yer bleedin' well stop yer bleedin' row?'

Out comes Mr Murdoe now, wearing a yellow prickly vest and his famous naval tattoes, his face covered with mauve ointment.

'Why don't you perishing women shut up? I'm on nights I tell you; I'm on nights.'

'He's on nights!'

'So's my Bob, but he sleeps at his sister's; says it's quieter there.'

The knocking doors close, one by one.

Grandad with Snails
Michael Baldwin

Mrs Jaffer's house was very still. She had a tree in her garden, a honeysuckle by the door with soot on its leaves, and the blinds were drawn. We did not wire her door, it was a waste of time. Once we had knocked for five minutes, rap, rap, rap, and shouted into her letterbox. Even posting dirt into her hall did not worry her. She stayed fast asleep upstairs. She was always asleep. Sometimes, in the afternoon, she came down in her nightdress, all yellow faced, to take her milk in. It was no use calling to her then. She only smiled and said, 'Thank you dearie – 'ave a cup of tea?' and held the door open for us. We used to run.

Electric Train

I very soon got tired of seeing my toy train run smugly round its little circle of rails. I began to contrive sensational accidents. I constructed bridges that led nowhere, but ended half-way over a deep ravine in a dangling rail from which the engine and tender would fall 'in a tangle of twisted metal', with spinning wheels and madly hissing clockwork. I imagined myself in a shattered carriage hanging over the edge of the broken bridge – it was always the Tay Bridge – and I would invent a grisly repertoire of groans, strangled screams, last gasps and dying prayers. The flames were creeping nearer. I was a woman with her new-born baby. I was trapped but the baby was free. Could I throw him into the river, and leave myself to be devoured by the flames? In the end I threw myself down with the child, and we were saved by my crinoline, which opened like a parachute.

Sorrows, Passions and
Alarms
James Kirkup

Serious Games

When I was nine years old, my very close friends and I used to go up to quarry wood pond with our jam jars and catch tadpoles or blackheads as we called them. We would all bring them home and leave them three or four days depending on whether they were good or bad ones.

After four days we would tip them out on to a stone and Steve, who was my closest friend, would kill them by dropping another stone on top or by cutting them in half. After killing them we put the stones with them on the compost heap, pretending it was a burial place like the Indians have.

After a week or so this stone would be brought down and a piece of black net would be dropped over this. In the week previous when the stone had been on the compost heap I had made a wooden coffin to hold the tadpoles. So after this I placed the stone in the coffin and buried it. Dandelions were placed on the grave and Jim, my cousin, conducted the burial service, in which we were all supposed to wear black.

One day while my mother was digging she found one of our graves and my brother gave us away. Did I get a telling off and my mother told all the mothers on our estate and every time I went out I was teased to death by them.

Age 13
Jacqueline
Thistlethwaite

People   People   People   People
People   People   People   People
People   People me People   People
People   People   People   People
People   People   People   People

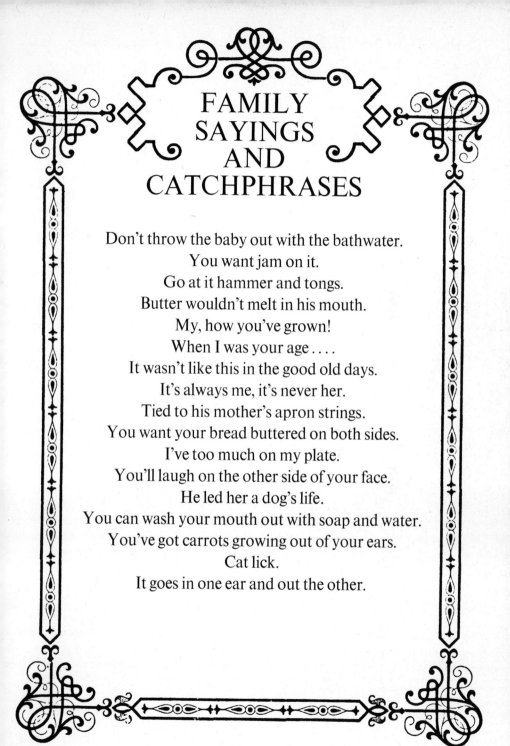

FAMILY SAYINGS AND CATCHPHRASES

Don't throw the baby out with the bathwater.

You want jam on it.

Go at it hammer and tongs.

Butter wouldn't melt in his mouth.

My, how you've grown!

When I was your age . . . .

It wasn't like this in the good old days.

It's always me, it's never her.

Tied to his mother's apron strings.

You want your bread buttered on both sides.

I've too much on my plate.

You'll laugh on the other side of your face.

He led her a dog's life.

You can wash your mouth out with soap and water.

You've got carrots growing out of your ears.

Cat lick.

It goes in one ear and out the other.

Where Do Babies Come From?

They squabbled endlessly about what I should be told. Father was for telling me nothing.

'But, Mick,' Mother would say earnestly, 'the child must learn.'

'He'll learn soon enough when he goes to school,' he snarled. 'Why do you be always at him, putting ideas into his head? Isn't he bad enough? I'd sooner the boy would grow up a bit natural.'

. . . Now one of the things I wanted badly to know was where babies came from, but this was something that no one seemed to be able to explain to me. When I asked Mother she got upset and talked about birds and flowers, and I decided that if she had ever known she must have forgotten it, and was ashamed to say so. Miss Cooney only smiled wistfully when I asked her and said, 'You'll know all about it soon enough, child.'

'But, Miss Cooney,' I said with great dignity, 'I have to know now. It's for my work, you see.'

. . . I appealed to my father and he told me that babies were dropped out of aeroplanes and if you caught one you could keep it. 'By parachute?' I asked, but he only looked pained and said, 'Oh, no, you don't want to start by spoiling them.' Afterwards, Mother took me aside again and explained that he was only joking. I went quite dotty with rage and told her that one of these days he would go too far with his jokes.

. . . At last I managed to detach the fact that mummies had an engine in their tummies and daddies had a starting-handle that made it work, and once it started it went on until it made a baby. That certainly explained a lot of things I had not understood up to this – for instance, why fathers were necessary and why Mother had buffers on her chest while Father had none. It made her almost as interesting as a locomotive, and for days, I went round deploring my own rotten luck that I wasn't a girl and couldn't have an engine and buffers of my own, instead of a measly old starting-handle like Father.

The Genius
Frank O'Connor

Fanta Immediately after breakfast my sister and I would start out, carrying our books and notebooks in a raffia satchel. On the way we would be joined by our friends, and the closer we got to school the more of us there would be. My sister walked with the girls, I stayed with the boys. Like all young boys we loved to tease the girls, but they gave as good as they got, and when we pulled their hair they fought back, scratching and biting us, although this did not dampen our enthusiasm noticeably. There was, however, a truce between my sister and myself; her friend, Fanta, also let me alone, but I did not return the compliment.

One day, when we were alone in the school yard, she asked me, 'Why do you pull my hair?'

'Because you're a girl.'

'I don't pull yours.'

I stopped to think for a moment. Only then did I realize that she was the only one, with the exception of my sister, who didn't.

'Well, why don't you?' I asked.

'Because!'

'Because! What kind of an answer's that?'

'I wouldn't hurt you, no matter what.'

'Well. I'm going to pull *your* hair.'

But then it seemed foolish to do it when none of my classmates was around. She burst into laughter when I did not carry out my threat.

'You just wait till school's out,' I threatened.

But again I did not make good my threat. Something restrained me, and from then on I hardly bothered her. My sister was not long in noticing this.

'I don't see you pulling Fanta's hair,' she said.

'Why should I? She leaves me alone.'

'Yes, I've noticed.'

'Then, why should I?'

'Oh, I don't know. I thought there might be some other reason.'

What was she getting at? I shrugged my shoulders. Girls were crazy; all girls were.

'Oh, Fanta makes me sick,' I said. 'And you make me sick too.'

She only laughed at me.

'Now, you watch out,' I said. 'If you don't stop laughing –'

She avoided my grasp and shouted from a distance: 'Fanta! Fanta!'

African Child
Camara Laye

Bickering

One of Sid's pleasures was to charge at the girls playing hopscotch on the pavement and kick away the stone that they pushed seriously one-legged from hell to heaven. When they saw him coming the girls ran away shrieking and from a safe distance called him nasty names and poked their tongues out at him. One afternoon a tall, fair girl didn't run away, but waited for him truculently. They met in the middle of the chalked oblong and there was a tussle. Sid got the stone and, wide trouser legs flapping, started to dribble it along the road. The girl ran after him, furiously scooping up dirt and pebbles from the gutter and hurling them at his back. Sid could run and dribble well, but he wasn't a bully, so he stopped to let the girl catch up with him.

'Say you're sorry,' the girl demanded.

'You're sorry,' Sid said.

'*Say you're sorry.*'

'You're sorry.'

The girl stamped her foot.

'Say . . . you're . . . sorry.'

'I *have* said it,' Sid sputtered.

'No you haven't.'

'Yes I have.'

'No you haven't!'

'You said say you're sorry and I said you're sorry. Didn't I?' Sid turned to me with an aggrieved expression.

'Didn't I?' he repeated appealingly.

The Railway Game
Clifford Dyment

'Yes,' I said, 'you did.'

Moving House 'Well thank goodness there aren't going to be any more children here anyway!' said Randy crossly. She spoke crossly because she was sad and she preferred sounding cross to sounding sorrowful, even though there was no one in the room except herself. Nobody and nothing, for that matter: her words had the particular ringing echo that is heard only in entirely empty rooms.

Almost all her life Randy had shared this room with her older sister Mona, and today they were going to go away and leave it. Forever. She looked carefully around because it is important to see clearly when one looks at something for the last time. How strange it seemed with all the furniture gone: smaller, somehow. In the long window the scarred shade hung crookedly as it always had: for hundreds and hundreds of nights its gentle flapping had been the last sound she heard before she slept. Goodbye, shade, thought Randy sentimentally. Randy sighed again and went out of the room for the last time. The last time: she'd been saying that to herself all day. She had paid a farewell visit to every single room in the house from the Office, which had been the Melendy children's playroom, to the furnace room in the basement. All of them looked bare and cold and friendless.

That morning the moving men had swarmed through the place, rolling up carpets, packing barrels, lumbering up and down the stairs with couches and chests of drawers on their backs like mammoth snails. Everything about the moving men was huge: their big striped aprons, their swelling necks and biceps, and their voices. Especially their voices; they had bawled at each other like giants shouting from mountaintops: 'GIVE US A HAND WITH THE PIANNA, AL', or 'CAREFUL OF THAT CORNER, JOE, DON'T KNOCK THEM CASTERS OFF'. But now they had gone, and all the furniture with them; swallowed up in two vans the size of two Noah's arks; and the house was an echoing shell, bereft and desolate.

Soon the painters and plasterers and carpenters would come into the house. They would patch up the ceiling, bolster up the sagging staircase, paint, and polish and mend till every sign of the Melendys was gone: the iodine stain on the base board, Randy's pictures, plasticine marks on the Office ceiling, the height-measuring marks of each Melendy child on the upstairs bathroom door, and all the dozens of other souvenirs left by four busy children in a home. The new people who had bought the house were old: a doctor and his wife. They were rich, too. How quiet the place would be under its new pelt of thick carpet. Old feet would go slowly up and down the stairs, doors would never slam, meals would be served on time by noiseless servants.

The Four-Storey
Mistake
Elizabeth Enright

Evacuated

I have this image of a small boy with a label tied round his neck. The boy has no features and is crying. He is carrying a cardboard box, which contains his gasmask.

I remember that labels with our names on were pinned to our clothes before we left London. I think I felt that I had no identity and was a parcel being posted to the country. The labels frightened me as much as the idea of leaving my parents. A child of seven, if lost, can tell people his name. A label assumes that he does not know his name, or worse, has no name and is given one at random from a list of names.

Perhaps the gasmask felt like a second face, a mask that would replace my own face as soon as I left London. I remember that the gasmask looked inhuman with its celluloid eyeshield and metal snout. I remember that it smelt of rubber and that I could not breathe properly inside it. The shield misted over with condensation and it felt warm and suffocating inside this second face.

I know that we rehearsed the evacuation every morning for a week. Each morning my sister and I would leave home with our packed sandwiches and clothes. We would say goodbye to our parents. Our labels were pinned on and I felt sick.

Mel Calman

Pretending to be Ill on Monday Morning

Monday morning found Tom Sawyer miserable. Monday morning always found him so, because it began another week's slow suffering in school . . . .

Tom lay thinking. Presently it occurred to him that he wished he was sick; then he could stay home from school. Here was a vague possibility. He canvassed his system. No ailment was found, and he investigated again. This time he thought he could detect colicky symptoms and he began to encourage them with considerable hope. But they soon grew feeble and presently died wholly away. He reflected further. Suddenly he discovered something. One of his upper front teeth was loose. This was lucky; he was about to begin to groan, as a 'starter' as he called it, when it occurred to him that if he came into court with that argument his aunt would pull it out, and that would hurt. So he thought he would hold the tooth in reserve for the present, and seek further . . . . So the boy eagerly drew his sore toe from under the sheet and held it up for inspection. But now he did not know the necessary symptoms. However, it seemed well worth while to chance it, so he fell to groaning with considerable spirit.

But Sid slept on, unsuspicious.

Tom groaned louder, and he fancied that he began to feel pain in the toe.

No result from Sid.

Tom was panting with his exertion by this time. He took a rest and then swelled himself up and fetched a succession of admirable groans.

Sid snored on.

Tom was aggravated. He said, 'Sid, Sid!' and shook him . . . .

Sid yawned, stretched, then brought himself up on his elbow with a snort and began to stare at Tom. Tom went on groaning. Sid said:

'Tom! say Tom!'

No response.

'Here Tom! Tom! What is the matter, Tom?'

Tom moaned out, 'Oh, don't Sid. Don't joggle me.'

'Why, what's the matter, TOM – I must call auntie.'

'No, never mind. It'll be over by and by, maybe. Don't call any body.'

'But I must! Don't groan so, Tom, it's awful. How long you been this way?'

'Hours. Ouch! Oh, don't stir so, Sid. You'll kill me.'

'Tom, why didn't you wake me sooner? Oh, Tom, don't! It makes my flesh crawl to hear you. Tom, what IS the matter?'

'I forgive you everything, Sid.' Groan.

Tom was suffering in reality now, so handsomely was his imagination working, and so his groans had gathered quite a genuine tone. Sid flew downstairs and said, 'Oh, Aunt Polly, come! Tom's dying!'

'Dying!'

'Yes'm. Don't wait, come quick!'

'Rubbage! I don't believe it!'

But she fled upstairs nevertheless, with Sid and Mary at her heels. And her face grew white, too, and her lips trembled. When she reached the bedside she gasped out: 'You Tom! Tom, what's the matter with you?'

'Oh, auntie, I'm –'

'What's the matter with you? – what IS the matter with you, child?'

'Oh, auntie, my sore toe's mortified!'

The old lady sank down into a chair and laughed a little, then she cried a little, then did both together. This restored her, and she said 'Tom what a turn you did give me. Now you shut up that nonsense and climb out of this.'

The groans ceased, and the pain vanished from the toe. The boy felt a little foolish, and he said: 'Aunt Polly, it *seemed* mortified, and it hurt so, I never minded my tooth at all.'

'Your tooth indeed!' What's the matter with your tooth?'

'One of them's loose, and it aches perfectly awful.'

'There, there now, don't begin that groaning again. Open your mouth. Well, your tooth *is* loose, but you're not going to die about that. Mary get me a silk thread, and a chunk of fire out of the kitchen.'

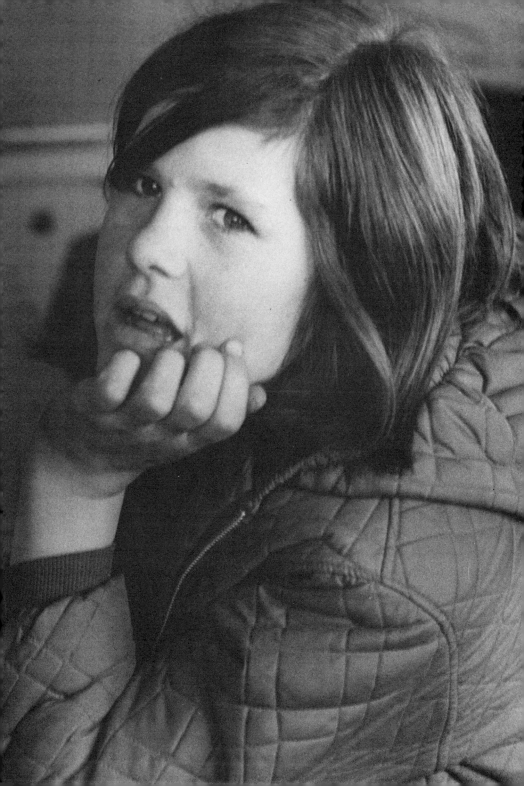

Tom said; 'Oh please Auntie, don't pull it out, it don't hurt any more. I wish I may never stir if it does. Please don't auntie; I don't want to stay home from school.'

'Oh, you don't, don't you? So all this row was because you thought you'd get to stay home from school and go a-fishing Tom? Tom, I love you so, and you seem to try every way you can to break my old heart with your outrageousness.'

By this time the dental instruments were ready. The old lady made one end of the silk thread fast to Tom's tooth with a loop and tied the other to the bed-post. Then she seized the chunk of fire and suddenly thrust it almost into the boy's face.

Tom Sawyer
Mark Twain The tooth hung dangling by the bed-post, now.

I've got a code id by doze,
An doebody doze
Traditional I've got a code id by doze.

It's not the cough that carries you off, it's the coffin they
Traditional carry you off in.

Burial Nobody wanted this infant born.
    Nobody wished it dead.
They wrapped it tight as an ear of corn
    In a box of cedar and lead.

Nobody by had lighted a candle;
    No one offered to moan.
The priest and I each lifted a handle.
    The father followed alone.

Three in a Ford, that had been waiting
    Most of the wintry day.
Boys on the river were skating;
    The wood and the road were gay:

Brown quick birds, and scarlet-berried
    Twigs, and snow begun.
The priest in the back seat sat and carried
    What never saw our sun.

A blanketed horse was at the gate,
    And someone's tracks led in.
We entered, and we ascended straight
    To where the graves were thin,

And where, on a hill, the digger bent
    In wind and thickening white.
Snow covered the box that two of us leant
    To lower out of the light.

Then priestly words to cover the snow;
    The four of us stood bare.
Then clods to keep those words below.
Mark Van Doren   Now there is nothing there.

Taking the Register
'Doreen Langley.'
'Yes, sir.'
'Ann Liddiard.'
'Present, sir.'
'Denise Murphy.'
'Yes, sir.'
'Felicity Murphy.'
'Yes, sir.'
'Are you two cousins? No? Related in any way?'
'No, sir.'
'Oh. Kate O'Reilly. Kate O'Reilly?'

'Absent, sir.'

'Sir, I saw her up Old Street yesterday with her mum.'

'Do you know why she isn't here?'

'No, sir.'

'Then there wasn't much point in telling me you saw her up Old Street yesterday with her mum, then, was there? Stella Riordan.'

'Here, sir.'

'Gladys Saintly.'

'Present.'

'Linda Salter.'

'Yes, sir.'

'Sonia Smith.'

'Here, sir.'

'Georgina Stoneham.'

'Here, sir.'

'Yvonne Stonehouse.'

'Here, sir.'

'Linda Taylor. Linda Taylor? Anyone know why Linda's away?'

'Please, sir, she's got fits.'

'She had one in class, sir.'

'She bit Mr Mackenzie, sir.'

'That's enough! Brenda Trussel.'

'Yes, sir.'

'Elaine Vaughan.'

'Yes, sir.'

'Lynn Waters.'

'Yes.'

'Now the boys. Christopher Arbor.'

'Yerp!'

You look hard at him. You decide to let him get away with it this time.

'David Bufton.'

'Yerp. Sir.'

Alan Burdick.'

'Yer-r-r-r-p!'

'Look, the next boy who tries to be funny while I'm calling the register is going to regret it. Georgiou Constantenou.'

'Yes, sir.'

'James Day. James Day?'

You will risk a joke.

'James Day seems away.'

B. S. Johnson   *Good, they laughed a little.*

First Day at School

But I was still shy and half paralysed when in the presence of a crowd, and my first day at the new school made me the laughing stock of the classroom. I was sent to the blackboard to write my name and address; I knew my name and address, knew how to write it, knew how to spell it; but standing at the blackboard with the eyes of the many girls and boys looking at my back made me freeze inside and I was unable to write a single letter.

'Write your name,' the teacher called to me.

I lifted the white chalk to the blackboard and, as I was about to write my mind went blank, empty; I could not remember my name, not even the first letter. Somebody giggled and I stiffened.

'Just forget us and write your name and address,' the teacher coaxed.

An impulse to write would flash through me, but my hand would refuse to move. The children began to titter and I flushed hotly.

'Don't you know your name?' the teacher asked.

I looked at her and could not answer. The teacher rose and walked to my side, smiling at me to give me confidence. She placed her hand tenderly upon my shoulder.

'What's your name?' she asked.

'Richard.' I whispered.

'Richard what?'

'Richard Wright.'

'Spell it.'

I spelled my name in a wild rush of letters, trying desperately to redeem my paralysing shyness.

'Spell it slowly so I can hear it,' she directed me.

I did.

'Now can you write?'

'Yes, ma'am.'

'Then write it.'

Again I turned to the blackboard and lifted my hand to write,

then I was blank and void within. I tried frantically to collect my senses but I could remember nothing. A sense of the girls and boys behind me filled me to the exclusion of everything. I realised how utterly I was failing and I grew weak and leaned my hot forehead against the cold blackboard. The room burst into a loud and prolonged laugh and my muscles froze.

'You may go to your seat,' the teacher said.

I sat and cursed myself. Why did I always appear so dumb when I was called to perform something in a crowd? I knew how to write as well as any pupil in the classroom, and no doubt I could read better than any of them, and I could talk fluently and expressively when I was sure of myself. Then why did strange faces make me freeze? I sat with my ears and neck burning, hearing the pupils whisper about me, hating myself, hating them.

Black Boy
Richard Wright

Assembly 'It's boring and Hypocritical. By Hypocritical I mean that by the prayers and things we do it's made out to be thanking God, but our assembly has nothing to do with God. It's cold, empty and utterly meaningless. I mean by this if it were a true service in dedication to God we wouldn't have to stop when the Hymn singing isn't loud enough because God doesn't mind how we sing. This assembly is all for show and nothing else.'
Girl at state school *Age 12*

'When the prefect reads no one listens to it. Their minds go wandering off. Besides most mornings we cannot hear it.'
Boy at state school *Age 12*

'If you open your mouth and the headmaster sees you, you have to stand up. When we go in we have to sit on the filthy floors and then they wonder why your clothes are mucky.'
Girl at state school *Age 12*

Sister Mary came to speak to us on Sunday. None of us knew what she would be like and when she came into Cavendish Hall on that warm sunny evening she held the attention of us all.

She took as her text a verse from 1 Corinthians xiii – 'love never faileth' – she spoke of her work in London among the sad homeless people, who had not something which we had – a happy home. I was impressed by her simplicity as she spoke of her courage in her work and God's guidance.

I was very moved by Sister Mary's talk, and I think it taught me a great deal about my dealings with other people.
Boy at prep school *Age 11*

I can see something of what community spirit is about and I respect it.
Boy at public school *Age 17*

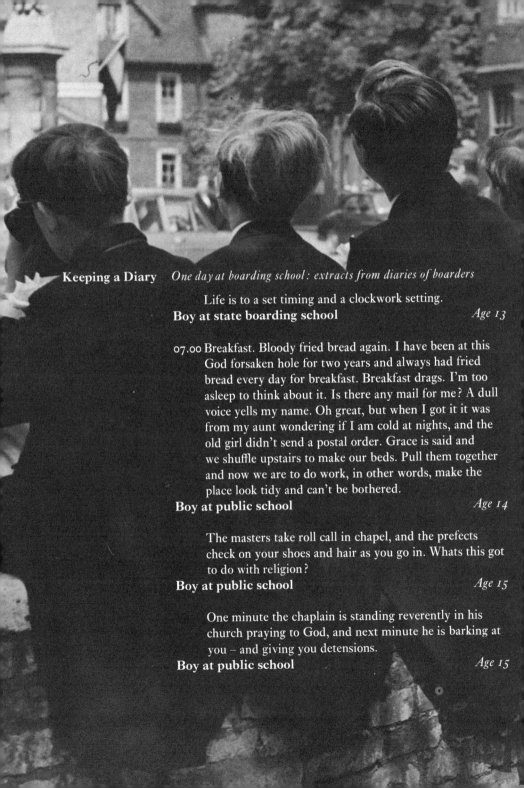

Keeping a Diary   *One day at boarding school: extracts from diaries of boarders*

Life is to a set timing and a clockwork setting.
Boy at state boarding school   *Age 13*

07.00 Breakfast. Bloody fried bread again. I have been at this
      God forsaken hole for two years and always had fried
      bread every day for breakfast. Breakfast drags. I'm too
      asleep to think about it. Is there any mail for me? A dull
      voice yells my name. Oh great, but when I got it it was
      from my aunt wondering if I am cold at nights, and the
      old girl didn't send a postal order. Grace is said and
      we shuffle upstairs to make our beds. Pull them together
      and now we are to do work, in other words, make the
      place look tidy and can't be bothered.
Boy at public school   *Age 14*

The masters take roll call in chapel, and the prefects
check on your shoes and hair as you go in. Whats this got
to do with religion?
Boy at public school   *Age 15*

One minute the chaplain is standing reverently in his
church praying to God, and next minute he is barking at
you – and giving you detensions.
Boy at public school   *Age 15*

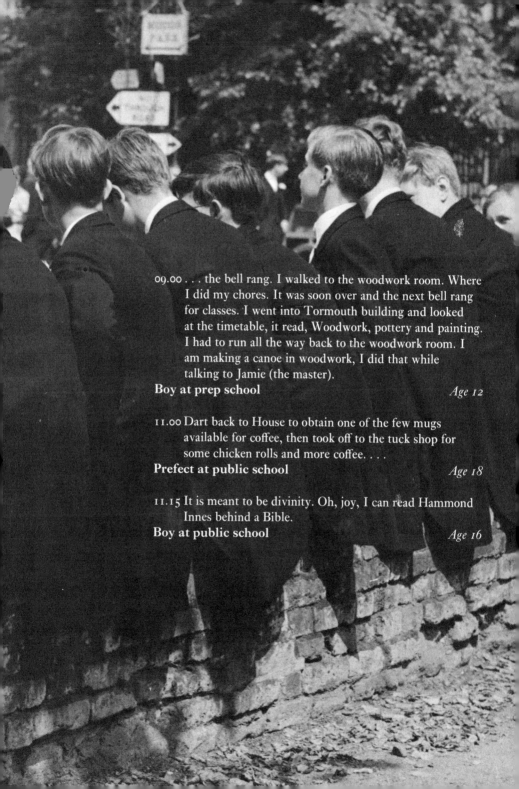

09.00 . . . the bell rang. I walked to the woodwork room. Where
I did my chores. It was soon over and the next bell rang
for classes. I went into Tormouth building and looked
at the timetable, it read, Woodwork, pottery and painting.
I had to run all the way back to the woodwork room. I
am making a canoe in woodwork, I did that while
talking to Jamie (the master).

Boy at prep school *Age 12*

11.00 Dart back to House to obtain one of the few mugs
available for coffee, then took off to the tuck shop for
some chicken rolls and more coffee. . . .

Prefect at public school *Age 18*

11.15 It is meant to be divinity. Oh, joy, I can read Hammond
Innes behind a Bible.

Boy at public school *Age 16*

12.30 When we were having dinner I told the first form boy across the table that my nickname was Kit so he quickly told the other form boys to call me Kitty Cat.

When I went to get the pudding Liz put salt in my water. When I came back I saw it looked a bit misty so I guessed and poured myself some more water. After dinner I tried to learn my french for a french test but I didn't succeed in learning very much.

Girl at Quaker school *Age 11*

2.00 Games. I had never played rugby before I came here. Similarly cross country, and although I hated cross country, it was a most enjoyable recreation compared to the misery of being sat in a puddle of smelly, foul and cold watery mud, with a grey sky, drizzle, and a cold N. Westerly wind blowing down the pitch, only a thin cotton shirt on one's back to merely distinguish you by colour (blue or white) by teams, no earthly use in keeping warm.

Boy at state boarding school *Age 18*

Anyone off games with a cold (or cough etc.) must wear a mac whenever he leaves the house. The games prefects have a list of such sufferers from Matron and check up the individuals daily. This intended to make colds as an excuse for being off games less pleasant and in the winter it succeeded.

Also no one with a cold may ride a bicycle.

Head of House's book at public school

4.00 Tea – jam sandwich – broken plastic spoon. 'Could you clear up that table please?'

Boy at progressive school *Age 17*

6.40 I have to take prep in the senior common room in the House which has about twenty people in it. After a few questions are asked, absolute silence is maintained.

Prefect at public school *Age 18*

8.00 Had some supper played the piano and came upstairs. Went round other Dorms talked to people in Bed and not in Bed. Came back to our dorm got undressed went and washed and did some washing. Got into bed at 8.55. Talked a bit and wrote my diary. Didn't curl my hair as

it's greasy and it doesn't curl when it is. Had some of
Anne's jelly in bed, strawberry (mmmmmmmmmmm).
Lights out at 9.15. Listened to my radio which is a
terrible crime if copped.

Girl at public school *Age 15*

Prayer. Thankyou, Lord, thankyou for giving me the leadership
of Hawthorn House; thankyou for my privileges and
my prefect's tie; for the house cup that we so closely
won and for the trust of the boys in my house, thankyou
Lord, thankyou.

Boy at prep school *Age 12*

Kiss Chase

The most striking episode in my primary school was our chases. These were spurred off by 'Petticoat Thursday' and 'Kissing Friday'. Most of us joined in the game. The object was to capture a girl and proceed to kiss her, or do some other suitable torture to her like taking her into the boys' lavatories and locking her in. The girls secretly liked being kissed by a boy. They used to scream and shout for help but when they were free they allowed themselves to be captured again. When no more girls came out we sent in scouts to send them out. The girls rushed out and we grabbed them. When the girls got fed up of being chased they chased us. It was horrible when they caught us. They gave us wet, sloppy kisses all over our faces. Sometimes the girls charge through our lavatories. This was invading our privacy so we threw them out. Although the kisses were wet we sometimes enjoyed this game.

Age 12
Paul Forster

Rythm

They dunno how it is. I smack a ball
right through the goals. But they dunno how the words
get muddled in my head, get tired somehow.
I look through the window, see. And there's a wall
I'd kick the ball against, just smack and smack.
Old Jerry he can't play, he don't know how,

not now at any rate. He's too flicking small.
See him in shorts, out in the crazy black.
Rythm, he says and ryme. See him at back.
He don't know nuthing about Law. He'd fall
flat on his face, just like a big sack,
when you're going down the wing, the wind behind you
and crossing into the goalmouth and they're roaring
the whole great crowd. They're up on their feet cheering.
The ball's at your feet and there it goes, just crack.
Old Jerry dives – the wrong way. And they're jearing
and I run to the centre and old Bash
jumps up and down, and I feel great, and wearing

Iain Crichton Smith   my gold and purpel strip, fresh from the wash.

True, Dare, Love, Kiss, Lick or Promise

A voice just outside suddenly said loudly, 'True, Dare, Love, Kiss, Lick or Promise?' I peeped out; she was addressing some girls lined up in front of her. I listened, fascinated. One of them answered, 'Lick.'

'Go and lick that girl under the arms.'

Uncomfortable pause. 'No.'

'Give me your shoe as a forfeit.'

'I'll have true,' said another voice.

'Is it true that you've just kissed the ground?'

The girl did so; I saw her. 'Yes.'

'Dare, please,' said another girl.

'Dare!' said the girl, who was It, gloatingly. She came and looked through the doorway at me. She really did look just like a rat.

'I dare you to go up to that girl,' pointing at me, 'pull up her dress, and pull down her knickers.' I screamed. To my intense relief the whistle went. The girl's face fell, but she made up for it by clinging on to the shoe.

Don't Knock the Corners Off
Caroline Glyn

'You can't have it back, you've got to win it back,' she said to her victim. They were still quarrelling about it on the stairs as I turned into my classroom.

Fight The whole school knew about the fight the next morning. I was a bit frightened in case any of the teachers got to know about it, but proud in a way because I was so famous. All day me and Raymond Garnett kept out of each other's way. I thought I could beat him with one hand tied behind my back, but as the day wore on I started getting like a sinking feeling and wanting to go to the lavatory all the time. I didn't want to go back to school after dinner and I wished I could break my leg.
But I knew I would have to go, and on the way back to school Ted shouted after me: 'Have you made your will out?' . . .

I walked slowly out of the classroom, down the corridor and out of the main entrance with 'BOYS' printed up over it in stone, through the half-closed trellis gates and into the playground. At first it looked as though the others had gone but then I saw them all standing up near the railings – Ted, Little Rayner, Mono and Raymond Garnett.

'Thought he wouldn't come out!' said Little Rayner.

'Has he got his coffin with him?' said Ted.

We walked out of the playground and round by Parkside towards the fighting field. We walked without saying anything. The only one who spoke was Ted who said: 'Got any chewy?' to Little Rayner, and that was the only thing that was said.

I was frightened when we got down on to the field, not by Raymond Garnett but by this big crowd of kids who had waited to see the fight. At the same time I was happy because they were waiting to see me and Raymond Garnett and nobody else.

There was a big ring of kids round the grey patch that was worn in the grass, where the fights were always held. They parted to let us through, and looking round I saw hundreds of other kids teeming on to the field after us, some of them running. Little Rayner shoves his way to the front, singing: 'Whipsey-diddle-de-dandy-dee,' this stupid song we had to learn at school. I had never had a fight before. I felt important and pleased at the crowds who were round us, none of them touching us but leaving it to us to have our fight.

'Back a bit,' I said, and I was right pleased when they moved back. I took off my coat and handed it to a kid I did not know. He took it and held it carefully over his arm, and this pleased me too.

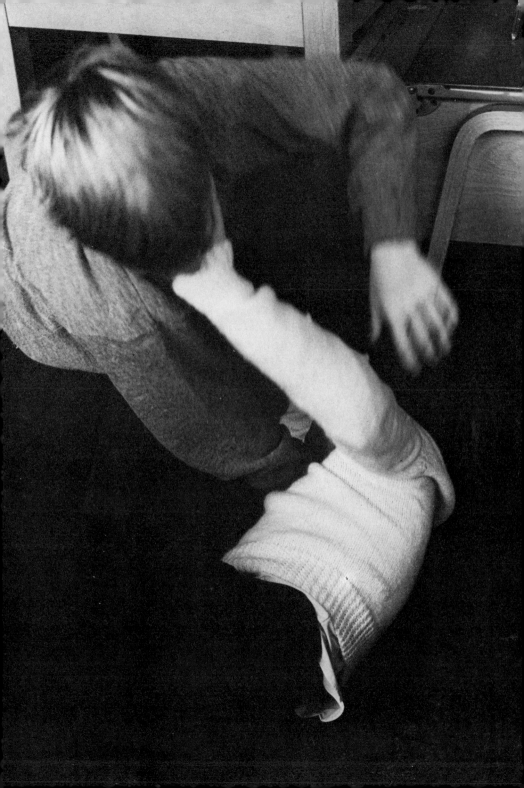

Raymond Garnett took off his coat and his glasses. I had never seen him without his glasses before, except that time when we were playing in Clarkson's woods with Marion. He had a white mark over his nose where he had taken them off and it gave me the feeling that I could bash him easy. He gave them to a kid to look after and as the crowd started pushing the kid went: 'MIND his glasses!'

We both stepped forward to meet each other and put our fists up. We stood staring at each other and dancing round a bit like they do on the pictures then I shot out my right hand to Garnett's chin but it missed and caught his shoulder. The next thing I knew was that his fist had caught me a stinging clout over the forehead. I was surprised and worried at the size of the blow and I began to notice, in a far-off sort of way, that he was a lot bigger than me and that his arms were thicker and longer.

I don't know how I got time to look at the people in the ring around us, but I did, and I noticed that I didn't even know most of them. Little Rayner was at the front shouting: 'Go it, Garno!' and this hurt me, don't ask my why. Ted was at the back, jumping up and down to get a good look.

I started trying to remember what people had told me about fighting. I knew you had to hit a man on his shoulders so as to weaken his arms, and another trick was to pretend to hit him in the belly and then when his arms went down, well you hit him in the face instead. They didn't work. I hit Garno twice on his right shoulder and he didn't feel anything, and when I tried to go for his belly my own arms were down and he hit me on the lip. I could feel it swelling already and I heard the crowd go: 'Ohhhh!' I suddenly realized that I had made a mistake and that Garno was tougher than I was and he was going to wipe the blinking floor with me and there was nothing I could do about it.

There is a Happy Land
Keith Waterhouse

Proverb   *He is a foole that makes a wedge of his fist.*

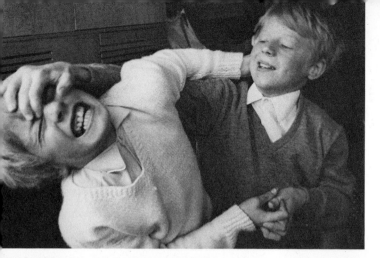

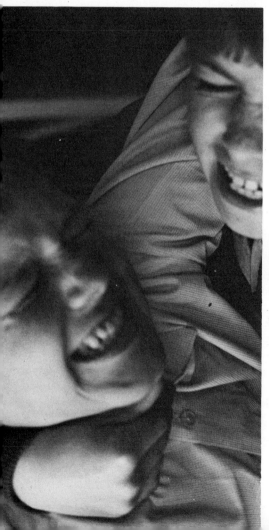

Maths Problem   *If it took five men one day to dig a field, how long would it take ten men to dig the same field?*

Discovery   We had one wonderful 'art' lesson, in which I learned to mix colours. We were given an oblong piece of white cartridge paper and a piece of red pastel. We had to lay the colour on very heavily at one end of the oblong, then use it more and more sparingly until, when we got to the other end, the paper was more or less white. Then – oh, mystery! – we were given a piece of yellow pastel, and told to use it as we had used the red, but starting at the opposite end of the oblong. I shall never forget my amazed delight when I found myself creating a new colour – orange. My excitement increased when I found that red and blue made purple, and blue and yellow made green. Then we were all told about the spectrum, and about primary and secondary colours, and in the next art lesson I made a very smudgy spectrum.

James Kirkup

Classroom of the 1930s   The classrooms were dull. They smelt of sand, disinfectant and chalky blackboard dusters. There was a sour chill in the cloak-rooms. The walls of some of the classrooms were made of varnished partitions through which you could hear the class next door stodging through the alphabet or the Lord's Prayer or Thirty Days hath September. On the walls hung religious pictures, maps of the Empire, a large calendar and the alphabet. On the window-sills were bulb vases of dark green glass, and a saucer or two with carrot-tops growing in them. . . . I learned to write, painfully gripping the thin ribbed shank of a new school pen by copying out dozens of times set phrases like 'Virtue is its own Reward'.

James Kirkup

Haiku   In the child's homework
Translated from the   A word he doesn't know –
Japanese by   And father's face.
Geoffrey Bownas and
Anthony Thwaite
Anonymous

Running Away　My father tried to help me with my homework. He sat hunched over a textbook and I stood by the arm-chair looking over his shoulder, struggling to follow his reasoning. The hands of the clock rushed round and hardly anything would be done. There were awful pauses, with my father sitting motionless, breathing heavily. I tried to bluff by agreeing with him, to try to hurry him on to an answer, but he kept catching me out.

'It's no good if you don't understand it,' he told me. 'How are you going to learn it like that?'

It was useless telling him that if I did not have most of the problems done or something on paper to show, I should be caned for laziness. He wanted me to understand them, once and for all. He was patient and thorough. I knew I would never understand compound interest and problems with trains travelling at different speeds in opposite directions.

In despair I would stare at my mother. If she was worried, uncertain of what to do, she flew into irritation. 'Help the lad,' she cried at my father. 'Can't you help him?'

'That's what I'm doing!' he shouted back. 'Trying to get him to grasp it!'

'There isn't time for all that. What d'you have to be so long-winded for? Just do them, do the bloody things. Oh, I wish I could do sums!'

'How about tomorrow night? He'll be in a mess again, won't he? He'll be back again tomorrow night, you daft—'

'Rubbish!' my mother cried.

I stood with a set face. It was finished now. My father had pushed the textbook off his knee and let the pencil drop. In the morning I should be caned.

I must have been twelve when I stayed away for six days one November because of more trouble with my homework.

My mother gave me the packet of sandwiches as usual and I put them in the satchel against the horrible exercise-books. I had finished two problems out of six, and even those were wrong. I did not know what I was going to do.

It was Monday morning. There was a soft drizzle blowing into my face. As I sat on the bicycle I felt the tiny drops of moisture catching in my eyelashes. I was alone. No one could help me.

Ahead of me, at the end of the street where I lived, the colours fluttered down the traffic lights, orange and then green. That was the way I went. Instead, I started to pedal in the opposite direction, towards the country.

I rode along in a queer, empty state. My crime was too ghastly to think about, yet it blotted everything else out. I should never be able to go back now, after this. There was no solution. I was cut off from the school, the teacher, my classmates, my mother and father, everybody.

I looked round and was startled because there was no longer a street, or any buildings. I was going across the common already. It seemed incredible. I had been travelling for over ten minutes without watching where I was going. I kept on, riding slowly. This was not the common near Memorial Road, but another one, where I had often played when I was at my first school. It had only happy associations.

The road let me out across the raw, scrubby ground, open and flat on either side, except for a few hollows choked with gorse and brambles. I was hardly conscious of pedalling. The wheels spun under me steadily, with the familiar clear knocking sound coming out of the bottom bearing, in the silence. The noise comforted me a little, banging away cheerfully, as if this were a normal journey.

Something made me turn the handle-bars suddenly to the right, and I bumped over the low kerb and started jolting along a faint track on the wintry grass. There were bare patches worn by boys playing cricket, and I noticed some charred pieces of wood in a circle of ash, left by a tramp.

Finally I stopped in a hollow. I sat for a long time in a stupor, all blank inside. The slight rain was almost finished. Drops had collected under the gorse bushes, hanging very still on the points.

After a while I got stiff, so I pushed up the little slope to level ground, then went on towards the aerodrome. How strange to be here now, on this grass where I used to play when I was careless, happy! All at once I felt desperately sorry for myself, lonely and cold, and I wanted to cry. The bitter tears came, hot on my face, which I knew looked haggard and old. I thought of the joy of owning a bicycle, the far-away happiness of summer days on the common, and how it had all ended in this. It was unbearable. I rode on, blindly staring until my front wheel hit a big jagged stone and I nearly fell off.

I was afraid to go back into streets, where people might notice me with my satchel. When I thought it was dinner-time I ate my sandwiches, sitting in a lane. At last I felt certain it had gone half-past four, and asked a woman going into a cottage. It was only three.

I rode as slowly as I could, in a wide circle, putting my brakes on down the hills. I came out on the road leading across the common, but a little farther away from the city than before. There were a few people now, sitting on benches or walking idly. Nearly all of them were elderly.

I kept asking the time from old men who had watchchains slung across their stomachs. They would be too tired to care what I was doing, I thought. The last one I asked had querulous, watery eyes with sore rims, and the skin of his huge hand around the watch was greyish-white. It looked as hoary as an elephant's hide, wrinkling and folding over, moving slowly.

I reached home at my usual time, just before five. Nobody seemed suspicious, and when my mother said: 'Have you got much homework tonight?' I almost believed for an instant that I had really been to school, that the whole day was a dream.

'Not too bad,' I answered.

I sat at the table casually, undid my satchel and pulled out the exercise-books. Spreading them out, then moving the pen over the pages as if I were writing, I realized how easy it was to deceive people sometimes: even your mother. A pang of shame went through me.

That night I lay awake a long time, trying to think of a way to spend the next day. It was too dreary on the common; I couldn't face it again. There were only the parks, I decided. Even they were no good if it rained. But in the morning the sky was clear, and while I sat eating my breakfast I remembered another place. I got my bicycle out of the shed and headed for the cemetery. I used to spend whole Sunday mornings there with my brother, chasing him down the muddy paths between the graves as our grandfather worked. He cut flowerstalks with some rusty scissors, and kept shouting at us to behave ourselves. There was a chapel which had dirty plaster flaking off it, and against one wall grew a monkey tree. It fascinated us. We stood on the chapel steps, closed our hands cautiously over the spikes on the ugly drooping branches and pretended we were going to swing. Or we ran with the tin containers to the tap, throwing away the bad water and filling them up. The time always flashed by.

Being alone was very different. As soon as I reached there I knew it would be hopeless, but I kept on because there was nowhere else far enough away to be safe.

In the clear space outside the gates there was a chestnut tree. I leaned my bicycle against its massive trunk and sauntered in past the lodge at the entrance, very conscious of the satchel bouncing impudently on my back. I had stuffed my cap in my raincoat pocket to as to look less like a schoolboy from the front. The lodge seemed empty, but I felt sure I was being watched by somebody inside, at one of the blank, curtainless windows sunk back in the ivy.

A woman hurried towards me on the gravel path, carrying a heavy iron watering-can, her face peevish. She did not appear to see me, and I was glad when she had gone past. She was the only person I saw, except for a figure stooping over stiffly in the distance, half hidden by a marble headstone.

I wandered about by the shabby chapel. It was so quiet everywhere, the air hanging dead over the trees, that I found myself listening to the sound of my bag as it bumped against my back. My feet made the only other noise, crunching through the silence. They sounded too confident to belong to me.

I soon grew desperate and longed for someone to come who would break the stagnant stillness. I took different turnings, tried to get lost among the paths, but kept coming back to the chapel.

The monkey tree was unchanged, yet all the attraction had gone out of it. I went close and stared at the branches. I did not want to touch them. The whole tree looked lifeless and ridiculous now, as if somebody had invented it and stuck it in the ground for a joke. The twiggy English trees made it unreal, more like a huge brush made of metal, its weird blackish arms sagging evenly, like tired springs.

I came out and got on my bicycle again. The time dragged terribly in there; I had to find something else. The clock over the lodge doorway was only an hour farther round.

Suddenly it began to rain, a steady pouring. At first I stood where I was against the chestnut tree, forgetting that it had shed its leaves. The rags and shreds of them were under my feet, in sodden lumps. I ran a short distance with my bicycle, propped it at the kerb and sheltered in the shallow porch of a house.

When the door was snatched open and a thin, staring man began to come out I walked across the pavement and rode away slowly, trying to look unconcerned.

The rain drove me into the shopping centre. I had remembered places like Woolworth's and Marks and Spencer's, where you could walk round all day without buying anything. I was pressing down the pedals eagerly, amazed that I had not thought of this before. There were endless things to look at, and I should be warm and dry. I raced over a bridge, glancing down at the bricked yards, the felt and wire-netting, of hen-houses, the waterlogged cabbages. The glittering, scented stores glowed in me like a paradise, as I concentrated on them.

The street I wanted was old, with disused tramlines embedded in the centre. I went bouncing over the cobbles. My front mudguard was loose; it shuddered and rattled. Then my heart seemed to give a great leap, as a boy of my own age ran across from one pavement to the other, ahead of me. But it was no one I knew.

Outside Woolworth's there was a steam-roller, trundling and shaking and hissing. I propped my bicycle just inside the mouth of the arcade, that went boring down in a long glass-roofed tunnel to the market, and stepped into my new refuge.

It was almost empty. After the bleak world outside, the gaudy interior blazing with light shone like a palace. I saw my face reflected in the wall of mirrors behind the weighing machine. It gave me a shock, the skin red from the rain and wind, the hair in a high, black mop. I clawed through the hair with my fingers, to flatten it.

A battering, man's voice was singing, filling the place with noise. I was grateful for it. My feet could clatter on the pale floor as much as they liked. The sight of the gleaming counters stretching into the distance, with girls posted along them, doing nothing, made me nervous at first. When I understood that no one was taking the slightest notice of me I began to wander happily, dazed by the tinsel glamour.

All the smells rose and mingled, pressing round, heavy in the air. I seemed to be pushing through them with my face, wave after wave of sweetness. I went along an avenue which had soaps and bath-salts on one side and loose banks of peanuts on the other. My eyes were tugged by the peanuts, even when I was well past.

Afterwards there was the problem of where to eat my sandwiches. I solved it by going down to the abandoned market. The stalls were all shuttered and forsaken on Tuesdays. In the open part, the tarpaulins held long lakes of water. It was still raining. I stood in a dry spot against the wall, where the roof of the big market building jutted out high overhead, and munched an apple. A lorry splashed in from the far end and curved towards me, so I retreated to the tunnel which had shops in its walls and a paved floor tilting gently to the street.

In Woolworth's once more, I kept noticing a ragged, strutting boy, younger and smaller than me. Another time I was in the British Home Stores, and looking across vacantly I spotted him jumping down a flight of steps.

The next day I saw him again, only a few yards away. As I hung my nose over the lamp-shades he sidled nearer, rubbing against the counter, until he was near enough to reach out and touch me. Still he did not speak. He waited for me to move away from the counter a little, then trotted up quickly.

'I saw you yesterday,' he said jauntily, grinning up.

'Yes, I saw you,' I answered, smiling.

He stared at my face to see if I were friendly.

'What's your name?' he asked bluntly.

I told him.

'I'm called Eddie,' he said. Then he added quickly: 'Don't you go to school?'

'Why?' I asked carefully.

He stood watching me.

'You playing truant, like me?' he asked, not grinning now. But he did not seem worried. He spoke as if he were asking me about my holidays. His face looked small, and sick. I liked his eyes. I was sure he wanted to be friends.

'Yes,' I admitted.

He nodded, matter of fact, then glanced round like a little general surveying things.

'I been away two weeks,' he boasted. 'How long you?'

'Only three days,' I told him. It sounded like an apology.

We were companions now. We stayed together for the rest of the day, and arranged to meet the next morning. It was wonderful having somebody to talk to. I meant to cling to him. I felt stronger already, and the fear hanging over me became vague and easily forgotten.

He mentioned a boat he was building for himself, out of bits of wood.

'Want to see it?'

'Where?' I asked curiously.

'Behind our house – at Clutton End. In the court at the back.'

Clutton End was a slum. A miserable trickle of rusty water, full of bricks and tyres, struggled into it under a bridge and followed the wall of a brewery, where the waste pipes dripped all the time. People laughed because such a degraded thing was still known as a river.

'All right,' I said.

Eddie became evasive.

'Not today, we can't,' he muttered. He looked down at his feet, kicking sullenly at a shop pillar. 'Tomorrow.'

But the following day, Friday, he was missing. I searched for him calmly at first, looking in all the places I could think of; even underground in the lavatory, near the market-hall clock. Down there it was freshly washed out, with no heavy smell. The attendant stood by himself, rubbing at brasswork on the yellowed tiles. I turned round and was climbing the damp steps as he raised his head.

Before long I was running from one store to another, afraid of missing Eddie and frantic at the thought of being left alone. There was no sign of him. On Monday the same thing happened, except that I was more hopeless and resigned, not really expecting him to turn up. I never saw him again.

That evening I sat at home with my books spread on the table, pretending to do homework. I had done the same thing night after night. This was my sixth day away, and no one in the house suspected.

The whole family was at home. Suddenly there was a weak
knock on the back door. My mother stood in the kitchen,
ironing, so she answered it, and I heard a high voice which I
recognized, saying very clearly:

'Excuse me, but the teacher would like to know when Paul is
coming back to school.'

Not daring to look up, I was aware of my father's head lifting
slowly. I heard his newspaper crackle as his hands clenched.
I was speechless with fright. The boy outside said politely:
'Sorry to have troubled you,' as if he had been rehearsing it,
and went away.

Then my mother came into the room.

'Oh dear,' she said in a low voice which was nearly a moan. She
stood tiredly in the doorway, staring at me. 'Oh, why didn't you
tell us, why ever didn't you tell us?' she cried pitifully.

My throat was working and thickening. Then my father stood
up violently, with a dark face.
'No, leave him, look,' my mother started to say quickly, but
before she could finish I burst into tears.

It was a great relief afterwards to be free of my awful secret,
but now the ordeal of going back and facing everyone in the
morning hung over me in its place.

Lying in bed that night I heard an argument going on in the
living-room underneath. At one point the stairs door crashed
open for some reason, and I heard my father's voice raised in
anger, with my mother, she must have been nearest the door,
crying out: 'It stands to reason he didn't do it for nothing!'

She took me back herself. As we came up to the school railings
at nine-thirty, and I heard one of the classes chanting something, I was overwhelmed with the horror of what I was doing.
I turned to my mother in such dumb misery, imploring her,
that she murmured distractedly: 'I can't help it, I've got to
take you back. Oh, I wish I could go instead!'

She asked to see the headmaster. Her timidity made it a
torment to her, having to face authority and put her feelings
into words. I knew how she was forcing herself forward by the
way she walked, holding her small figure too stiffly.

I was made to wait outside the door of the little office. When it
opened, I was amazed to see the stocky headmaster's smiling

face and my mother obviously relieved.

'Leave Paul to us, will you?' he said in a false voice, patting my mother's shoulder. 'I promise you we shan't punish him, or bring the matter up in any way, after what you've told me.'

She nodded, thanked him, and left without glancing at me again. For a moment, seeing her hurrying away across the bleak

playground, I felt horribly lost and delivered over to my tormentors. The headmaster had made himself charming and friendly, and my mother had been glad to believe that my fears were all exaggerated, I thought wildly. How treacherous adults were! I wanted to run madly, in any direction, to hide in a dark place and never be found.

Philip Callow

COLLECTIONS

B. S. Johnson

And there we went nesting, finding few, and other boys telling us they had fried blackies' and thrushes' eggs in a cocoa tin lid over a wood fire, they were just a mouthful, they said: I was repelled by the thought, they might have been addled, or had partly grown young birds in them. It did not seem cruel to me, nesting, I did not think of it as in any way cruel, no.

Keith Waterhouse

We went collecting tram tickets and added up the numbers to see what our fortunes were. One for sorrow, two for joy, three for a letter, four for a boy. I was a three. What you had to do, you had to add up all the figures on the tram ticket together and see what's left over. Marion showed me how to do that. She knew a lot, did Marion. It was her that told me that if you swallow chewing gum, well it gets all tangled up round your heart, and if you swallow orange pips, well you get oranges growing out of your ears.

For a while I kept black-and-yellow striped caterpillars. I put them first of all in match-boxes with bits of cabbage and lettuce leaf. Pin holes were pierced in the lids. The smell of the decaying leaves and the caterpillar droppings was pungent, savage. I was secretly terrified of the little ramping, champing monsters, and couldn't bear to handle them. I was dismayed, when, opening one of the match boxes too hastily, the caterpillar, which had been clinging to the lid, instead of curling up into a little rubber tyre, allowed itself to be squashed. It was at school: my cry of 'Mlaa!' was heard all over the classroom.

Then I got a shoe box to keep some hairy caterpillars in. I removed the lid, and gummed some muslin over the top so that I could see what was going on. I placed the box in the sun in the bay window, and went off to afternoon school. I came running eagerly home to look at my pets but found they had eaten through the muslin and were crawling up the front-room curtains. My mother, who was sitting sewing in the window, hadn't noticed their escape until one dropped on the back of her neck. I had the horrible task of picking the furry critters off the lace curtains and throwing them into the garden. That was the end of my career as a caterpillar fancier.

James Kirkup

You played with fag cards against the school wall, out in the street, you sat on the pavement skimming the cards and feeling sharp pangs of loss if you got beaten, and it was the same pavement outside your own house, just down the street. Everything was joined on, continuous. You played marbles in the gutter, going nearly all the way home like that, measuring and aiming and rolling the magic striped glass, eyes glued to the cobbles, and the gutter ended at the drain under the lamp-post opposite the entry which sliced down the side of your house.

Philip Callow

One of the nurses at the hospital had given me a book on natural history. But I didn't like the book, because it wasn't about animals moving but about animals that were dead. To me, nature study meant life, but to the author of this book it meant collecting. He told you how to treacle trees to catch moths, how to make a killing bottle for your captured butterflies, how to examine the contents of shot birds' stomachs. There was one passage about preserving caterpillars, that made me vomit whenever I read it. 'Lay a full grown caterpillar on a sheet of blotting paper,' the author instructed, 'and turn the blotting paper around until the caterpillar is crawling away from you. Place a pencil on the caterpillar firmly, just behind the head, and roll it towards the tail. This kills the creature instantly, and presses its internal organs out through the anal orifice. Roll the pencil over once or twice again, to make sure that all the contents of the body are emptied out, then insert a blow-pipe into the anal orifice, hold in a hot air oven, and applying your mouth to the blowpipe

Clifford Dyment inflate the caterpillar gently. . . .'

Punishment Children streamed out of the classrooms and rushed rowdily down the corridor. Miss Dabbott's voice could be heard ordering them to walk properly, and from the classroom behind the Head's study Mr Gubb appeared with a cane in his hand.

'Everyone stand still!' he bellowed. Only a few obeyed.

'Keep still all of you!' he shouted again, in a tone which none could fail to hear. This time the children nearest to him slouched to a standstill, but the others continued moving and chattering. As he strode forward to deal with them, a small boy ran out of the cloakroom, chased by a bigger one, and both blindly collided with him. He gasped with pain as the head of the smaller boy caught him in the stomach.

'You blasted idiots!' he cried; and, as they cowered back against the wall, he seized them by their shirt collars and shook them furiously. This action, and the ominous appearance of Mr Jenks, caused a cessation of movement.

Mr Jenks marched along the corridor, glaring wrathfully about him, and the children fell back on both sides without a murmur.

Mr Gubb, his round face crimson with anger, was still shaking the two major culprits.

'You two have asked for it,' he growled, 'and now you're going to get it!' He pushed them away from him. 'Hold out your hands. Both of you!' he added, when only the bigger boy obeyed. 'I hope this will be a warning to them all,' he observed to Mr Jenks, who stood grimly watching the scene at the end of the corridor.

The bigger boy was the first to be punished. He was a stocky, curly-headed lad of about thirteen. He extended his left hand, but the position was not to Mr Gubb's liking.

'Get your hand higher up,' he commanded, tapping the boy's knuckles with the cane.

The boy raised his arm a few inches higher.

'Now stretch your fingers right out, unless you really want to get hurt.'

The boy stretched his fingers to their furthest limit and held his thumb back rigidly, at right-angles to his forefinger. He stood erect with his head thrown back, his chin jutting upwards, his mouth twitching slightly in fear, but his jaw set in defiance and

bravado, as John had seen men look when clumsy hands, working without anaesthetics, had probed to extract shell-splinters from their limbs. The boy's eyes were fixed on the master. He did not budge as Mr Gubb raised the cane above his shoulder and fixed his eyes on the boy's fingers with the concentration of a golfer addressing his ball. Only when the cane cracked down across his hand did the boy's nerve fail. In that moment he blinked, jerked back his head, blenched, contorted his lips, and then, as the shock was absorbed, the splinter tugged free of the flesh, his body relaxed and he casually lowered his arm. Yet his apparent unconcern was belied when he turned away from the children and cupped his hands tightly together behind him.

'Get the other hand up,' Mr Gubb directed the smaller boy, an untidy, unhealthy looking lad. 'Don't you know which is the right one yet?'

The boy lowered his arm, but instead of raising the other he looked abjectly away from Mr Gubb, and began to cry.

'What's the matter with you?' demanded Mr Gubb. 'Can't you take your medicine? Hold up your hand or worse will be coming to you.'

The boy sniffled and stammered to say something, but the words would not come.

Mr Gubb tapped his knuckles with the cane. 'Get a move on,' he said menacingly. 'Stop behaving like a girl. I haven't got time to waste on you.'

Still the boy made no effort to obey, but only sobbed the louder. His shoulders heaved and his chest shook with sobs. His nose began to water, and the grime from his lips was carried slowly downwards by the fluid in two, dirty streams which he made no effort to check.

Complete silence had fallen on the children. None of them moved. They stood tensely watching, their attention fixed on the boy. Mr Gubb made an angry move forward and seized his arm.

'If you don't do it yourself, I'll have to do it for you.'

As he straightened the boy's fingers there was a stir amongst the children, and a voice, which John knew at once to be Harkness's, called out, urgently and angrily: 'Leave my brother alone! He's got a bad hand, sir!'

Mr Gubb dropped the boy's hand and looked up at Harkness.

'Who asked you to interfere?' he snapped.

'Nobody,' Harkness answered, coming forward, 'but he's been to hospital with that hand, and if you cane him on it, he'll have to go again.'

'What's supposed to be wrong with it?'

'He had a splinter in it. It went septic, and it's not better yet.'

'If that's the case,' said Mr Gubb, turning to the victim, 'why didn't you tell me before?'

The tension in the corridor eased. John hoped that Mr Gubb would now spare the boy: but there was to be no remission; the penalty had to be paid, the example given.

'Put the other hand up,' ordered Mr Gubb.

Still sobbing, but not so wretchedly as before, the boy raised his right arm.

'This is one I hope you'll remember,' said Mr Gubb. He measured his distance, took up his stance, waved the cane twice above his shoulder and brought it briskly down. But before he had completed his swing the boy fearfully withdrew his arm and the cane rapped harmlessly on the floor.

'This is the last time,' Mr Gubb warned. 'If you do that again, I'll . . .'

'I think you'd better leave him for now,' interrupted Mr Jenks, walking down the corridor, 'I'll deal with him later.'

'I'll give him one last chance,' said Mr Gubb. He prodded the boy in the chest with the cane. 'Are you going to take it from me, or would you sooner have it from Mr Jenks?'

Without replying, the boy sniffed miserably and raised his arm. This time there was no mistake. Despite his sobs, the boy's hand remained steady. As he received the blow his face writhed and he gasped with pain. His body doubled forward and he stumbled against the wall, wringing his hands together between his knees.

Mr Gubb addressed the children, holding the cane erect against his shoulder, like a rifle. 'Let that be a lesson to you all. Don't let me catch anybody else rushing about the corridor, or they'll know what to expect. Now let me see you all get outside quietly – without any talking at all.'

Michael Croft

The Desk Lid I looked at the desk lid in wonder;
Thinking of all the kids who had sat there,
Thinking of all the pens that had touched there,
Wondering what weather had passed there
Even thinking of teachers that had taught them,

Age 11 I wonder what lesson the person was having

Fay Lawrenson When he had written 'I am me'.

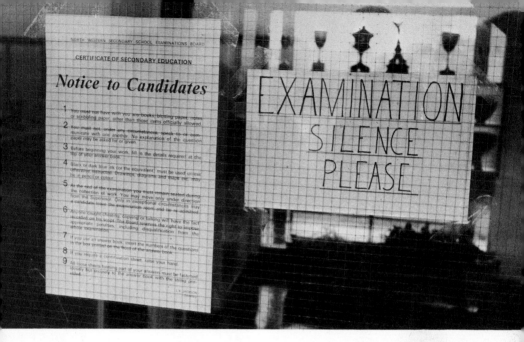

Examination   The classroom was very quiet. The twelve o'clock buzzer had gone, and all who were not taking the examination had gone to dinner. So had many of the candidates. Either because they had done as much as they could do, or like their fathers and mothers did not like the sense of being separated from their friends and fellows, most of the young examinees had handed in their papers and gone. Once outside the school they ran off into the streets like fish returned to the stream. Only a handful of boys was now left, and the only sounds in the room were the gurgling of the pipes, the scraping of hobnail boots on the iron crosspieces of the desks, and the scratching of pens. As the minutes ticked by, one more candidate gave in, and his rough boots clattered over the floor of the classroom as he went up to hand in his paper. In the end there was only one boy left. When he looked up and found he was alone he felt a momentary pang of alarm. He was too engrossed to be seriously troubled, but he must have looked a little anxious because the teacher stirred and spoke. It was Mr Cresswell, a teacher whom the boys generally feared. He was irritable and impatient and at times violent. Yet when he spoke it was in a kind voice. 'Don't hurry, Kirtley. The examination goes on until half past. You have plenty of time left.'

It was a pleasant surprise to hear him speak in so gentle a voice, and the boy was suddenly inspired with a tremendous

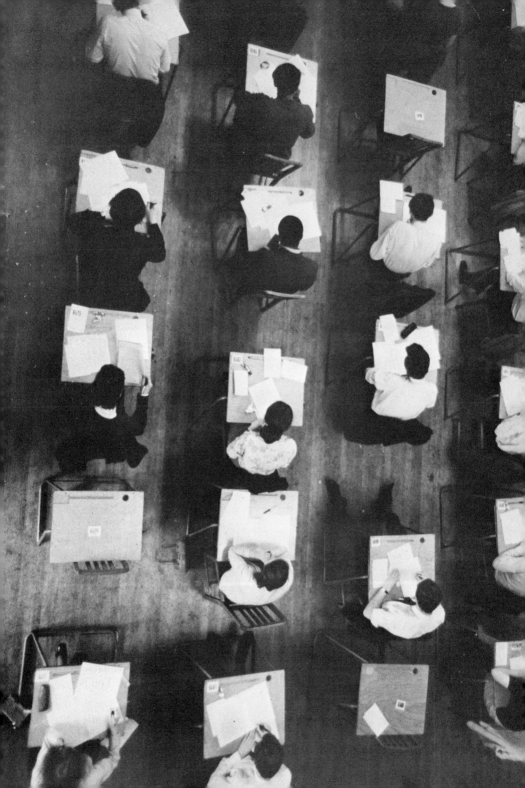

resolution, almost with obstinacy. He would not be rushed. He hadn't finished yet, but there was nothing wrong in not having finished. The time was still his and he was determined to use it.

He worked quickly, looking up from time to time. In these little intervals he did not seem to observe anything, yet everything imprinted itself upon his brain – the old stained map on the wall, so dark and brown that hardly any detail could be seen on it, the queer grain, like contour lines, on the cheap yellow cupboards, the long cobwebs hanging from the high ceiling, and Mr Cresswell's bent right arm, the arm that had been damaged in the war. He looked down and returned to the last questions.

'Write down in your own words the meaning of the following proverbs: "A rolling stone gathers no moss." . . .'

It was difficult to find new words for that, but he wrestled with his vocabulary and found an equivalent. He struggled with all the proverbs and as the hand on the discoloured school clock moved towards the half-hour, he ruled off and gave in his paper. There was a moment of solitude as he stood, the only boy in the great empty playground, but he pulled on his cap, kicked a stone before him, and ran home.

As he drew near to home he could hear the familiar sounds of a colliery washing day – the thumping of the poss-sticks in the wash tubs, a rhythmic boom-boom as the wooden possers beat against the bottom of the tubs; and when he turned the corner he saw the lines of washing all strung out across the muddy streets. One of those poss-sticks being pounded up and down in the tub and one of those lines belonged to his mother.

When he got home he found her in a kitchen full of steam and the unpleasant odour of washing. The floor was covered with piles of dirty clothes, all sorted into whites and coloureds; and every flat space was occupied by her paraphernalia – scrubbing-brushes, tins of blue, bowls of starch, slabs of yellow soap, and pegs. Francis's mother was always in a disagreeable mood on washing-day; she was even more cross at his coming home at this inconvenient time.

'A nice day to pick for an examination, I must say,' she said. 'You would have thought they'd have enough sense to keep off a washing day, at any rate. Well, you'll have to slip down to Mrs Cairns', and get yourself a pie and a few peas, because I canna be bothered with you.'

The Oak and the Ash
Frederick Grice

First School Dinner There were lots of oilcloth-topped tables and low chairs from the kindergarten. A strange woman in a white dressing-gown was arranging us at the tables. She stood me at a table beside Skinner. There were more women dressed like her dishing up brown stuff from a great cauldron through a hatchway. Some villainous-looking boys I didn't know came and stood next to Skinner, shepherded by the woman. The din was quite incredible. We were all screaming at the top of our voices. I found myself shouting too, for no reason. At the end of the room stood Miss Lovely on a wooden platform. She was shouting as well, quite inaudibly. The cooks were fussing around like nannies. They stood a boy I recognized from Class One beside me on the other side, and then Felicity Dearchild, and then O'Brien. They were all yelling hard.

Suddenly Miss Lovely rang a bell. Screaming more loudly than ever, everyone ran across the room and stood against the wall opposite the hatch. I followed, and was almost squashed to a pulp between Dearchild and one of the ruffianly looking boys. They had all got plates from somewhere. I looked wildly round. All I could see was a pile of broken vegetable dishes beside one of the hatches. When my part of the queue arrived there I snatched a bit of one and held that through the hatch. The cook didn't notice. She put a bit of pastry on it that might or might not have meat underneath, and then to my horror, half emptied a bottle of ketchup over it. I grabbed it away. The ketchup ran off the broken edge of the dish all over my dress. I went back to my place next to Skinner hating Daddy for making me have school lunches, and thinking what I would say to him at home.

Miss Lovely blew a whistle. That seemed to be the signal for us to scream a shade less loudly. At least, by looking at her mouth, I could make out what she was saying.

'Benedictus benedicat per Jesum Christum dominum nostrum,' said Miss Lovely very slowly, 'Amen.'

I looked at my plate. The pastry had disappeared, and there was only a bit of meat and some unattractive gristle. As I looked across Dearchild leant across, yelling, speared the meat with her fork and put it on her own plate. I looked at my own plate disbelievingly. One of the boys flicked a large lump of fat across the table on to it. I sat down on the tiny chair, thinking it was as well that I wasn't hungry. My head came just above the table. O'Brien and Skinner, who I had always thought were no bigger than me, didn't seem to have any trouble.

'Whee! Smash!' shouted one of the boys rushing his mug of water across the table and spilling it into my ketchup. 'Watch out! It's the Ferrari 216. Whoo!'

I said to the boy from Class One next to me,

'I suppose you've just been taking your eleven plus. What did you think of it?'

He punched me in the face.

Miss Lovely rang a bell. All the children jumped on to their chairs and put their hands on their heads.

'Now, silence, please!' she said. She checked us on the lunch register. 'All right, get on.'

We all screamed and got down again. Instead of sitting down and finishing, however, we took our plates and rushed to queue at the hatches, still eating. I followed. We queued for ages. By the time they reached the hatch the others had finished and were served out some more, but I had no intention of eating their leftovers that they had dumped on my plate, and was sent back in disgrace.

'Go on! You haven't finished. You can't have anything more till you do,' said the cook. I went back to my place and waited till the rest of my table had eaten their second and third helpings. It took a long time because they kept taking things off each other's plates and fighting and playing cars with the water mugs. Twice Miss Lovely rang a bell for silence. . . . At last they finished, and the cook came to clear away the plates. Inside the hatches I could see piles of some steaming pudding which the cooks were dousing with treacle. It really didn't look too bad. I began to feel almost hungry.

Don't Knock the Corners Off
Caroline Glyn

'Just look at that! You haven't eaten a mouthful,' said the cook, poking at my cold gristle. 'Now you're just going to sit there till you finish it, if it takes you all night.' She stood beside me and made me do it while the rest ate the pudding.

School Language

Names for tapioca and sago

Fishes' eyes
Frogs' eyes
Fishes' eyes in glue
Frog spawn
Wallpaper paste
Baby food

An Injection   We stampede down the corridor,
Each holding a white card.
Fingering it like some poisonous insect.
Will it hurt?
The thud of our feet echoes our drumming hearts.
'Bags last!'
'I'm going last.'
'I'm not going first.'
'Me neither.'
We stand in line,
Like prisoners waiting for execution.
I'm not scared.
I try to sound heroic.
I drift . . .
Into a senseless dream.
I snap out of it as my friend jolts me,
Saying, 'Go on, it's you next.'
I march stiffly towards the door.
The nurse motions me to the chair.
The saliva refuses to enter my mouth.
The blue-flamed bunsen burner hisses slightly.
The drab, grey walls seem more depressing than usual.
My sleeve is pushed roughly up.
The strong stench of disinfectant bites my nostrils.
My arm is touched with something cold.
I shudder violently.
It brushes my arm
Soothingly.
Everyone falls silent.
It's over!
A mere pin prick.
A bubble of blood
Dribbles down my arm.
It's absorbed by a piece of lint.
A gush of breath rushes out.
The air seems clearer.

Age 12   My mind fresher.
Janet Clark   'Next please.'

Conundrum   *What is the difference between a lazy schoolboy and a
fisherman?*

Home and School Questionnaire

Put a tick in the box if your answer is 'yes' and a cross
if your answer is 'no'

1 Where do you feel most at ease?
   a. at home ☐
   b. at school ☐
   c. out with your friends ☐

2 Should boys do as much housework as girls? ☐

3 How much pocket money do you get each week? _____
   How much *should* you get? _____

4 Should schoolchildren be allowed to do part-time jobs? ☐

5 If you have a weekend job should you get money from
   home as well? ☐

6 What time do you stay out until?
   a. during the week _____
   b. at weekends _____

7 Is there any favouritism in your family? ☐

8 Where should grandparents live?
   a. with their families ☐
   b. by themselves ☐

9 Do you mainly obey your parents' wishes over the
   following issues?
   a. clothes ☐
   b. choice of friends ☐
   c. hair ☐
   d. where you go ☐

10 If your parents allow you to have pets
    a. do you look after them yourself? ☐
    b. do your parents help you? ☐

11 Should uniform be worn in schools? ☐
    If so, outline briefly your model uniform

    _____

    _____

12 Should girls and boys be taught
   a. in mixed classes? ☐
   b. separately? ☐

13 Is the discipline in your school
   a. too strict? ☐
   b. too slack? ☐

14 Who should have a say in the running of the school
   and the making of the school rules?
   a. everyone in the school ☐
   b. only the headmaster, staff and prefects ☐

15 Should senior forms have more privileges than
   junior forms? ☐

16 If you were headmaster in your school what
   improvements would you like to see made?

   _____

   _____

17 Do you think school dinners are good value for money? ☐
   (Find out how much money the school cook has at her
   disposal and what regulations she has to obey)

18 If you were showing a visitor round your school what
   aspects of the school would you point out?

   _____

   _____

19 Is homework necessary? ☐
   If so, how much time should be spent on it each night?

   _____

20 What reasons would you give for doing the following
   subjects at school?
   a. physical education
   _____
   b. woodwork
   _____
   c. music
   _____
   d. metalwork
   _____
   e. domestic science
   _____
   f. drama
   _____

In watchful community

In watchful community
when we ought to be at school

sheltering by the warehouse
we stand, smelling
creosote, and the musty
rot of wood from floorboards
where sacks have lain, for
years, huddled together.

That is behind us, but
in front we hear the
plop of rain, and
while we stand
our bodies are increasing
in secret society.

Thom Gunn

'Richard Ullathorne! Ullathorne! Where is he? Ah, yes.
Mr Allcroft wants to see you. Come on, lad. Don't look
thunderstruck. Get a move on.'

Dick started up from his seat in great fear. If the Chief
Constable or the Public Executioner had sent for him he could
not have been more alarmed. There passed quickly through his
mind all the misdeeds of which he could remember being guilty
in the last few weeks – climbing on the school wall, copying
from Jo Basey, shouting down the steps at the boiler man,
flashing a mirror in the music lesson. If the headmaster wanted
to see him, it was, of course, to cane him. He expected to be
caned, and began to wonder how many he would get. He put
his hand in his pocket, took out from a tin the horsehair that he
had pulled out of his grandmother's settee, and wrapped it
furtively round the middle finger of his right hand. Jo Basey
said it would make the cane split.

The headmaster looked at him over his glasses, and blew twice
down his nostrils. He always gave two little snorts like this, as
though he was preparing to charge.

'Are you Richard Ullathorne?'

'Yes, sir.'

'Why isn't your brother Christopher at school?'

'I don't know, sir.'

'What do you mean by saying you don't know? He is your
brother, isn't he?'

'Yes, sir.'

'You both live at the same address, don't you?'

'Yes, sir.'

'Well, don't be obstinate, boy. What's the matter with him?'

'Please, sir, I don't know, sir. I haven't seen him since last
Wednesday.'

'You haven't seen him? You must have a big house if one
member of the family never sees the other. Where do you live?'

'Twenty-three Chapel Row, sir.'

'That's not exactly a mansion, is it?'

Richard did not reply.

'What are you holding your tongue for, boy?'

'Please, sir, I'm not sure what a mansion is.'

'Well you should be. You've read the Bible, haven't you? "In my Father's house are many mansions." Have you never heard that verse? A mansion is a large house. What are you frowning at?'

'I can't understand it, sir. I can't understand how a house can have large houses in it.'

'What? Now, don't be argumentative, Ullathorne. Where's this brother of yours? You know he's playing truant don't you?'

'Please, sir, he's gone off somewhere.'

The Bonnie Pit Laddie
Frederick Grice

'Yes, but where?'

'Please, sir, we don't know.'

Owning Up

Others made darts of penholders and nibs, fixing paper tails to the split extremities, and hurling them into the dimness of the ceiling, where some stuck. Others covered tennis balls with ink, and bounced them against the white walls of the hall, leaving what they termed 'spugs' upon their surfaces. Periodically Mr Rore would demand the names of any culprits who had thrown a ball, but without success.

Once, indeed, after a scornfully terse address by the Head, one boy had stood up and admitted that he had thrown a ball. He was congratulated for his 'sense of honour', and informed that his 'Spartan attitude was so worthy that he should welcome punishment'. The boy was caned, but on returning to the Hall all he said was: 'I never damn well thought he'd give me the whack, or I wouldn't have owned up like a fool.'

The Beautiful Years
Henry Williamson

Sneak

Tell tale tit,
Your tongue shall be slit,
And all the dogs in the town
Shall have a little bit.

Traditional

Telling Tales   I still remember – my hands and finger tips still remember! – what used to lie in store for us on our return to school from the holidays. The guava trees in the schoolyard would be in full leaf again, and the old leaves would be strewn around in scattered heaps. In places there were even more than just heaps of them: it would be like a muddy sea of leaves.

'Get that all swept up!' the headmaster would tell us. 'I want the whole place cleaned up, at once!'

'At once!' There was enough work there, damned hard work, too, to last us for over a week. Especially since the only tools with which we were provided were our hands, our fingers, our nails.

'Now see it's done properly, and be quick about it,' the headmaster would say to the older pupils, 'or you'll have to answer for it!'

So at an order from the older boys we would all line up like peasants about to reap or glean a field, and we would set to work like members of a chain-gang. In the schoolyard itself it wasn't too bad: the guava trees were fairly well spaced; but there was one part where the closely-planted trees grew in a hopeless tangle of leaves and branches. The sun could not penetrate here, and the acrid stench of decay lingered in the undergrowth even at the height of summer.

If the work was not going as quickly as the headmaster expected, the big boys, instead of giving us a helping hand, used to find it simpler to whip us with branches pulled from the trees. Now guava wood is regrettably flexible; skilfully handled, the springy switches used to whistle piercingly, and fall like flails of fire on our backsides. Our flesh stung and smarted, while tears of anguish sprang from our eyes and splashed on the rotting leaves at our feet.

Occasionally, one of us, worn out by such calculated cruelty, would have the courage to complain to the headmaster. He would of course be very angry, but the punishment he inflicted on the older boys was always negligible – nothing compared to what they had done to us. And the fact is that however much we complained, our situation did not improve in the slightest. Perhaps we should have let our parents know what was going on, but somehow we never dreamed of doing so; I don't know whether it was loyalty or pride that kept us silent, but I can see now that we were foolish to keep quiet about it, for such beatings were utterly foreign to our nature, to the most fundamental and secret principles of our character, and completely at variance with our passion for independence and equality.

But one day, one of my little school-mates, Kouyate Karamoko, who had just been brutally assaulted, declared openly that he had had enough of this sort of thing.

'Yes, I've had enough of it!' he said to me, sniffing through his tears. 'D'you hear? I've had enough! I'm going to tell my father.'

'You keep quiet,' I said. 'Telling your father won't do us any good.'

'Do you really believe that?'

'Don't forget, the big boys . . .'

But he would not let me finish.

'I'm going to tell him,' he cried.

'Hush, don't shout like that!'

We were working in the same row, and he was the nearest to me in it: I was afraid that this outburst would bring another flogging from the big boys.

'You know what sort of man my father is, don't you?' he said.

'Yes, of course.'

Kouyate's father was one of the most venerated praise-singers of the district. He was an educated man, welcome everywhere, though he no longer practised his art; he was a kind of emeritus praise-singer, and very proud of his position.

'But your father's an old man now,' I said.

'He's tough!' said Kouyate proudly.

He drew his thin little body up to its full height.

'You make me laugh sometimes!' I said.

Whereupon he began to whimper again.

'Oh, well, do as you like!' I told him.

The next day, Kouyate had no sooner entered the schoolyard then he went over to Himourana, the big boy who had thrashed him so mercilessly the day before.

'My father is most anxious to meet the boy who has been kindest to me in the top class, and I thought of you at once. Can you come and share our dinner this evening?'

'You bet I can!' answered Himourana, who was as stupid as he was brutal, and probably as greedy as he was stupid.

That evening, at the appointed time, this big bully Himourana showed up at Kouyate's compound. Now this compound is one of the best-guarded ones in Kouroussa: it has only one gate, and the fence around it, instead of being made of woven reeds, is constructed of mud bricks with pieces of broken glass bottles fixed to the top. It could be entered and left only with the permission of the master of the house. Kouyate's father came in person to open the gate, and when Himourana was inside, he carefully bolted it.

'Would you care to sit down in the courtyard?' he said. 'Our whole family is expecting you.'

Himourana took a quick look at the pots and pans, which seemed to give ample promise of a succulent repast, and sat down with the rest of the family, eager for the compliments that he felt sure were about to be addressed to him. But Kouyate got up and pointed at him.

'My father,' he said, 'this is the big boy who never stops beating me, and takes my food and my money!'

'Well, well,' said Kouyate's father, 'that's not a nice thing to say about him. Are you sure you're telling the truth?'

'I swear by Allah!' said Kouyate.

'So it must be the truth,' said his father.

And he turned towards Himourana.

'Well, young man, it's time you gave an explanation of your strange behaviour. Have you anything to say in your defence? Be quick: I haven't much time to spare, but I don't want to be uncharitable.'

It was as if a thunderbolt had dropped at Himourana's feet – he could not have been more dumbfounded: he had obviously not heard a word of what Kouyate's father had said to him. As soon as he had recovered a little from his surprise, his one thought was to get away; this was obviously his best course, but it needed a stupid bully like Himourana to imagine he could escape from such a well-guarded compound. He had not run more than a few steps before he was caught.

'Now, sir,' said Kouyate's father, 'Listen carefully to what I
have to say to you; get this into your head, once and for all:
I do not send my son to school to learn how to become the
slave of boys like you!'

And thereupon Himourana felt himself lifted in the air by
his feet and arms – everything had been carefully planned – and
held in a convenient position, while, despite his screams,
Kouyate's father laid into him, belabouring his bare backside
with his cattle whip. Then he was allowed to run away,
shamefaced, with his tail on fire like a scalded cat.

Next day, the story of Himourana's beating spread like wildfire.
It created a real scandal. Nothing like that had ever happened
before, so that we found it hard to realize that it had actually
taken place, although we all felt we had been avenged by the
action taken by Kouyate's father. The big boys of the two top
classes held a meeting and decided that Kouyate as well as his
sister Mariama would be sent to Coventry, and they ordered all
of us to send them to Coventry too; but they did not dare lay a
finger on Kouyate or his sister, and at this even the stupidest
among us became aware that they were afraid: we suddenly felt
that an era had ended and we prepared to breathe the air of
liberty again.

At midday, I went up to Kouyate, having decided to defy the
big boys' orders.

African Child
Camara Laye

'Careful,' said Kouyate; 'they might beat you for this.'

'I'm not afraid of them!' I said.

School Thief   MISS TILLINGS Somebody in this room is a thief!

[Silence]

MISS TILLINGS Somebody – some wicked, wicked child – has stolen our lovely daffodil.

CLASS Aaah!

MISS TILLINGS Yes, our lovely daffodil. The one we've all watered and tended since the middle of March. Sit absolutely *still* every single one of you. Quite, quite still! I have my own ways of finding nasty little sneak-thieves.

[A long pause. Miss Tillings stares hard round the class. The children try to keep their composure, scared of any movement which might be interpreted as guilt. Suddenly Nigel can bear it no longer and his hands go up to his face]

MISS TILLINGS Stand up Nigel Barton!

[Nigel stands, head bowed in shame]

MISS TILLINGS Well, Nigel! Do you know anything about this? I can't believe it was you!

[At this last sentence, Nigel looks up, a faint hope glimmering]

NIGEL No, Miss.

MISS TILLINGS Then what do you know about it?

NIGEL I think – I think I might have had the daffodil, Miss.

MISS TILLINGS *[Sharp] Might* have had it? What do you mean, boy! Come on, speak up.

NIGEL *[Twisting his head round]* I – I . . .

MISS TILLINGS *[Menacingly] Well?*

NIGEL The stem was all broke, Miss. Somebody – somebody – *gave* it to me, Miss.

MISS TILLINGS *Who* gave it to you?

NIGEL Um. I don't like to say, Miss . . .

MISS TILLINGS You better had, Barton! And be quick about it!

NIGEL Georgie Pringle, Miss.

CLASS Aaaah!

[Georgie jerks up in indignant astonishment]

PRINGLE I never did!

MISS TILLINGS Quiet Pringle! *[She advances on Nigel almost cooing]* All right Nigel. Thank you. And where did Pringle give you this broken flower?

NIGEL By the bus stop, Miss. The stem was all broken. I thought I'd try to mend it.

PRINGLE It's a lie! A lie!

MISS TILLINGS You'd better be quiet, Pringle! Does anybody else know anything about this? Did anyone see Pringle with the flower? Anyone see him come back into the school last night?

FIRST BOY I saw him go back into the school, Miss.

PRINGLE No, Miss no!

MISS TILLINGS Quiet! Did you see him come out again?

FIRST BOY *[Regretfully]* N-no.

[The children sense blood and start to get nasty. There is an air of excitement. Eyes are gleaming]

MISS TILLINGS *Somebody* must have seen him come out again. What about you, Bert. Or are you mixed up in it too?

BERT *[Alarmed]* No, Miss. Not me, Miss.

MISS TILLINGS Well? Was he with you? Did you see him come out?

[Bert is nervous. He shoots glances at Georgie]

BERT Y-yes, Miss. He wasn't with *me*, Miss. I did see him come out, I mean.

[Class lets out a deep sigh of satisfaction]

MISS TILLINGS *[Quickly]* And he had the daffodil in his hand, didn't he? Didn't he!

BERT Yes, Miss.

PRINGLE No, Bert! No!

BERT In his left hand.

GIRL I saw him too, Miss.

MISS TILLINGS Where did you see him?

GIRL *[Looking round for applause]* By the bread shop, Miss. And him had the daffodil, Miss. The stem was all broke, like Nigel says.

MISS TILLINGS Come out to the front, Georgie Pringle!

PRINGLE *[Tearful]* It ent true, none of it, Miss.

MISS TILLINGS Come out to the front! *[Gently]* All right, Nigel, you can sit down now. Thank you for being so truthful.

Dennis Potter NIGEL *[Smirk]* Thank you, Miss.

The End of School
Age 12
Colin Chapman

Bell rings, boys run, doors slam,
distant feet in the playground;
only the silent steps of the cleaners.

Answers to Puzzles and Riddles

Acknowledgements

For permission to use copyright material acknowledgement is made to the following:

Poems and Prose

For 'Door Knocking' from *Grandad with Snails* by Michael Baldwin to Routledge & Kegan Paul Ltd; for 'In the child's homework' and 'Making her doll' translated by Geoffrey Bownas and Anthony Thwaite from *The Penguin Book of Japanese Verse* to Penguin Books Ltd; for 'Crazes' from *Going to the Moon* by Philip Callow to MacGibbon & Kee Ltd; for 'Collections' and 'Running Away' from *Native Ground* by Philip Callow to William Heinemann Ltd; for 'Evacuated' by Mel Calman from *The Evacuees* edited by B. S. Johnson to Victor Gollancz Ltd; for 'Seeing a Parent Cry for the First Time' by Carole Carr to the author; for 'The End of School' by Colin Chapman to the author; for 'An Injection' by Janet Clark to the author; for 'Punishment' from *Spare the Rod* by Michael Croft to the Longman Group Ltd; for 'Bickering', 'Collections' and 'Crazes' from *The Railway Game* by Clifford Dyment to J. M. Dent & Sons Ltd; for 'Moving House' from *The Four-Storey Mistake* by Elizabeth Enright to William Heinemann Ltd and Holt, Rinehart & Winston Inc.; for 'Kiss Chase' by Paul Forster to the author; for 'What a Blessing Younger Brothers Are' by Catherine Frankland to the author; for 'First School Dinner' from *Don't Knock the Corners Off* by Caroline Glyn to Victor Gollancz Ltd; for 'Examination' from *The Oak and the Ash* by Frederick Grice and 'Visit to the Headmaster' from *The Bonnie Pit Laddie* by Frederick Grice to the Oxford University Press; for 'In watchful community' from *Positives* by Thom Gunn to Faber & Faber Ltd; for 'Five Green Bottles' from *Five Green Bottles* by Ray Jenkins to Margaret Ramsey Ltd; for 'Crazes' from *Trawl* by B. S. Johnson to Secker & Warburg Ltd; for 'Taking the Register' from *Albert Angelo* by B. S. Johnson to the author; for 'Classroom of the 1930s', 'Collections', 'Cupboard under the Stairs', 'Discovery' and 'Electric Train' from *Sorrows, Passions and Alarms* by James Kirkup to Collins Publishers; for 'Keeping a Diary' from *The Hothouse Society* by Royston Lambert to George Weidenfeld & Nicolson Ltd; for 'The Desk Lid' by Fay Lawrenson to the author; for 'Fanta' and 'Telling Tales' from *Dark Child* by Camara Laye to Collins Publishers; for 'Birth' from *A Roof Over Your Head* by Bill Naughton to Blackie & Sons Ltd; for 'The Vacuum' from *New and Selected Poems* by Howard Nemerov to Faber & Faber Ltd and the University of Chicago Press; for 'Where Do Babies Come From?' from 'The Genius' from *Domestic Relations* by Frank O'Connor to A. D. Peters & Co.; for 'School Thief' from *Nigel Barton Plays* by Dennis Potter to the author; for 'Spilling Soup' from *Call It Sleep* by Henry Roth to Michael Joseph Ltd; for 'Slippery' from *Smoke and Steel* by Carl Sandburg to Harcourt, Brace & World Inc.; for 'Rhythm' from *The Law and the Grace* by Iain Crichton Smith to Eyre & Spottiswoode (Publishers) Ltd; for 'Crazes' from *'What Have You Been Doing?'*

List of Illustrations

Index of Subjects

Index of Authors, Translators and Collectors